English in Medicine

Third Edition

English in Medicine

A course in communication skills

Eric H. Glendinning
Beverly A. S. Holmström

CAMBRIDGE UNIVERSITY PRESS
Cambridge, New York, Melbourne, Madrid, Cape Town, Singapore, São Paulo

Cambridge University Press
The Edinburgh Building, Cambridge CB2 2RU, UK

www.cambridge.org
Information on this title: www.cambridge.org/9780521606660

First published 1987
Second Edition 1998
Third Edition 2005
3rd printing 2005

Printed in the United Kingdom at the University Press, Cambridge

A catalogue record for this publication is available from the British Library

ISBN-13 978-0-521-60666-0 Coursebook
ISBN-10 0-521-60666-7 Coursebook

ISBN-13 978-0-521-60668-4 Audio CD
ISBN-10 0-521-60668-3 Audio CD

ISBN-13 978-0-521-60667-7 Audio Cassette
ISBN-10 0-521-60667-5 Audio Cassette

Contents

Thanks

We again acknowledge our debt to the medical profession, in particular to Dr Vera Hogg and Dr Sheila Glendinning for their advice on updating the medical content of this edition and to Dr Jean Braun, Dr Evelyn Byrne, Mrs Maureen MacGregor SRN, Dr Richard Taylor, Professor James Walker, and Dr Alan Spence Watson for their help with earlier editions.

Comments from the classroom are particularly valued and we are grateful to both students and teachers who have given their views on the first edition.

Our thanks go to those who have helped in the production of this new edition, including James Richardson who produced the new recordings, Suzanne Williams who carried out the picture research, Marie Allan who cleared the text permissions, Jo Barker who designed the cover, Ruth Carim who did the proofreading, and Tony Robinson who did the content editing.

We would especially like to thank our editor, Annemarie Young, for thoroughness, good counsel and good humour throughout.

From the first edition

This book could not have been written without the considerable help of members of the medical profession. We acknowledge in particular the great debt we owe to Sheila Glendinning MB, ChB and Dr Alan Spence Watson for giving up so much of their precious free time to advise on medical content throughout the production of this book.

For additional help with materials and advice on case histories, warm thanks are due to Dr Evelyn Byrne MRCP, Dr Jean Braun MD, Mrs Maureen MacGregor SRN, Emeritus Professor James Walker, Rebecca Tomlinson of the BMA London, Sindy Leung, and Michael Holmström.

A special thanks is also due to Pat Coulter for typing the many drafts, to Dr Hamish Watson for his encouragement and comments on the final manuscript, and to our editor, Desmond O'Sullivan.

To the many overseas doctors, medical students, nurses and others who have worked through the successive drafts of these materials with good humour, we offer sincere thanks for all the suggestions and practical advice.

Finally, past and present teachers of the Edinburgh Language Foundation deserve our gratitude for their helpful comments. In particular we would like to thank Helen Mantell, Helen Tyrrell, Anne Rowe and Claire MacGregor.

To the teacher

This book is for doctors, medical students in the clinical phase of their studies and other medical professionals who have to use English to communicate with patients and their relatives and with medical colleagues.

It aims to develop speaking and listening skills primarily but attention is also given to reading skills, in particular the use of reference materials and journal articles. Practice is also provided in writing referral letters and completing a range of medical documents.

The book is divided into seven units, each focusing on one area of doctor–patient communication from history-taking to treatment. With the exception of Unit 7, which deals with different forms of treatment, all units have four sections. Section 1 introduces new language related to the unit theme. Section 2 provides further practice and introduces a variety of medical documents. Section 3 focuses on reading and Section 4 brings together the language studied earlier in the unit in the context of a case history which runs from Unit 1 to 6.

This book is the product of many years' teaching. It has been used successfully both by those with long experience in teaching English for Medical Purposes and by those new to this area of teaching.

Medicine is a field where innovation and development are constant. The specialist content in this third edition has been revised to reflect these advances, particularly in treatment. Work on online databases has been included, specialist texts updated and websites included in the list of useful addresses.

The histories, based on authentic cases and drawn from a range of specialisms as diverse as obstetrics, ophthalmology and neurology, have been updated to take into account developments in investigation techniques and treatment. All reference texts and journal articles have been replaced with the most up-to-date versions. Tasks have been coded according to the main skill developed (Listening, Reading, Speaking, Writing) and a number of activities have been restructured and resequenced. New photographs have been added to illustrate the themes covered in each unit and to provide extra teaching context. Finally, the list of useful addresses has been updated and the new UK hospital doctor gradings included.

The organisation of the book and the objectives of each type of activity are explained in more detail in 'To the student'. A specialist knowledge of medicine is not required, but you do require an interest in the language needs of the medical professions and a grasp of communicative and post-communicative teaching techniques. You provide the teaching expertise; the learner provides the medical knowledge. The right blend will give results. With a little practice, you can devise supplementary activities of your own based on the models in this book. See page 147 for ideas for such activities. Be creative and you will get the most out of this book and from your teaching.

To the student

This book aims to help you communicate in English with patients and their relatives, with medical colleagues, and with paramedical staff. It is also designed to help you cope with medical reading of all kinds from case notes to journal articles. Those of you who are medical students will find this book useful in the clinical phase of your studies. The authors have cooperated closely with members of the medical profession in preparing this book to ensure authenticity. They have long experience in helping overseas medical personnel with their communicative needs.

The book is divided into seven units. The units are sequenced to match your own dealings with a patient. You start with the English needed for consultations and continue with examinations – both general and specialist. Next you study the language required to discuss investigations, diagnoses and treatment both with the patient and with English-speaking colleagues. Finally you examine the English of treatment – medical, surgical and physiotherapy.

The first six units have four sections. The first section introduces new language and provides practice activities in a medical context. The second practises further language items on the same general themes and includes listening and writing practice involving medical documents. The third deals with reading skills and aims to develop the skills needed to understand a range of medical texts including hospital documents, textbooks, reference materials and articles. The final section consolidates the material covered in the first two sections in the context of a continuing case history which provides a link from unit to unit. Unit 7 has three sections on different forms of treatment and a final reading section focusing on using an online database.

The language activities in this book are coded according to the main skill developed.

Listening tasks

The listening passages include simulated doctor–patient interviews, a discussion among doctors, a phone call from a hospital laboratory and a physiotherapist giving instructions to a patient.

The tasks are varied but all have at least two of these stages: *before-listening*, *while-listening* and *after-listening*. In the *before-listening* stage you may be asked, for example, to predict the questions a doctor will use in an interview, or the order in which the doctor will ask about systems, or simply to fill in the gaps in a dialogue.

While-listening activities often involve comparing your predictions with the actual words used on the recording or taking notes from a consultation. Frequently you will be asked to complete an authentic document using information from the recording. Sometimes you are asked to concentrate on the *form* of the answer, the exact words used or the intonation pattern of the speaker.

After-listening activities focus on using the information you have obtained from the recording. For example, you may be asked to decide which department a patient should be referred to or to complete a referral letter.

If you are working alone, you can try this approach:

1 Try to do as much of the activity as you can without the recording. Guess the answers when you cannot be sure. This will help you to focus your listening on any problems which remain. In addition, it will narrow down the possible meanings when you listen.
2 Listen to the recording to check your answers and to fill in any gaps. Listen to sections you cannot understand as often as you like.
3 Turn to the Tapescript and listen to the recording again with its help.

Speaking tasks

The speaking tasks focus on speaking English in all aspects of patient care. Most of these tasks ask you to work with a partner, and some ask you to explain to your teacher or group the words you would use in particular situations.

The speaking tasks for pairs include: guided-practice activities with word or picture cues, information-gap activities which require the exchange of data to complete a form or to solve a problem, opinion-gap activities where you must justify your choice of investigation or the diagnosis you make to your partner, and role-plays: doctor–patient, doctor–relative and doctor–doctor.

The guided-practice activities are relatively simple as most of the words you require are provided. Make sure that you and your partner have the chance to play both parts. If you finish the activity ahead of time, try to add other examples of your own.

The gap activities require as a first step careful reading or listening to acquire information and to understand the situation. Then you are asked to exchange your findings with your partner. Make sure you exchange your data and ideas orally. There is no point in simply exchanging written answers so that your partner can copy them down. Once you have completed the exchange, read the text or study the diagram your partner has used. That way you can check that you have understood your partner correctly and that your partner has given you accurate information.

For the role-plays, your teacher may ask you first to prepare your role with another student. This gives you the chance to work out together the language to use and to anticipate what the other role-player will say so that you can respond appropriately. You will then be asked to play the role with a new partner. If time allows, exchange roles and repeat the task so that both you and your partner have the chance to play both parts. Some of the role-plays have been recorded so that you can compare your performance with those of native speakers. The recording is a guide and does not provide the only correct way to perform the roles.

In all these activities, there will be times when you do not understand your partner or your partner does not understand you. Making yourself understood in such situations is an important part of acquiring a language. Ask your partner to clarify or repeat points you do not understand. Repeat and rephrase if your partner cannot understand you.

If you are working alone, obviously it is difficult to have meaningful speaking practice. This does not mean that you should omit these activities. Speak aloud the parts, playing both roles where required. Then compare your performance with the recording. Stop the recording after each phrase, and try to repeat it using the same pronunciation and intonation as the speaker. Refer to the Tapescript for help.

Reading tasks 

Reading quickly and accurately are important skills for medical professionals. The reading tasks focus on practising reading strategies to develop these skills.

The reading passages include: a case history, textbook extracts, a pharmacology reference, extracts from journal articles and a wide variety of medical documents. All the texts are authentic.

Reading activities cover: locating specific information in a case history, transferring information from a text to a table or a medical document such as a form or a letter, completing the gaps in a text, identifying relevant sections of medical articles and using an online database.

As with listening, the reading activities have at least two of these stages: *before-*, *while-* and *after-reading*. In the *before-reading* stage you may be asked to list the main features of two similar medical problems. In the *while-reading* stage you read two passages from textbooks to see whether your answers are correct. In the *after-reading* stage you compare your list to decide which are the key features for differentiating between the problems.

If you are working alone, you can try this approach:

1 Using whatever clues are provided, the text title for example, try to anticipate what the text will contain. Read a sample of the text to help you.
2 Read the text to check your answers and to fill in any gaps. Note how long it takes you to find all the answers or to complete the task.
3 Check your answers with the Key (p. 105). Where your answers differ from the Key, reread the appropriate sections of the text.

Writing tasks

Many of the activities whose main focus is on other skills also involve writing. When you listen to the recording or read a passage, you may be asked to write notes. Writing is an authentic response to the listening or reading text.

Activities which focus mainly on writing include letters of referral and a discharge summary. There are no special problems or special approach needed for those of you who are working on your own. Attempt the task and check your answers with the Key in the normal way.

Language focus

Throughout the book there are brief comments on key language items introduced by the tasks, starting with basic questions. The focus is on the language used in medical communication. Grammar points without medical relevance are not included.

Appendices

Appendix 1 provides a checklist of the most useful language functions in medical communication.
Appendix 2 lists common medical abbreviations, both UK and US, and includes all abbreviations used in this book.
Appendices 3 and 4 explain who's who in the UK hospital system and UK and US grades.
Appendix 5 lists addresses of professional bodies in the UK and USA.

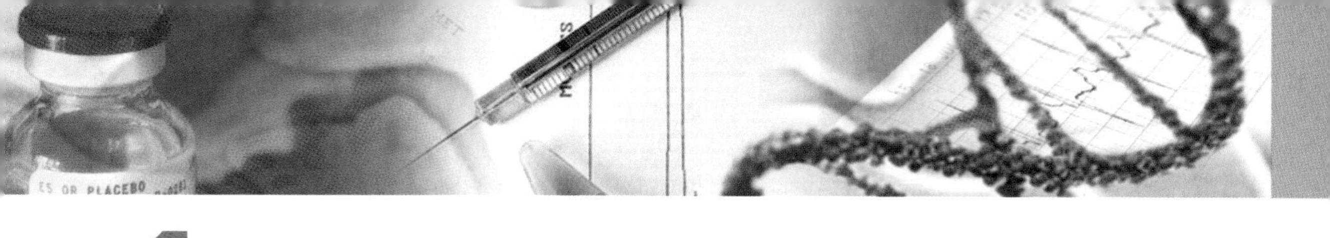

1 Taking a history 1

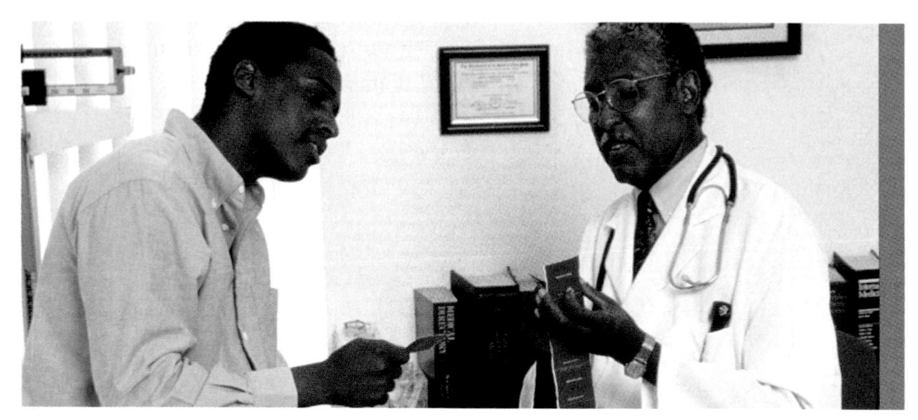

Section 1 Asking basic questions

Task 1

You will hear an extract from an interview between a doctor and his patient. As you listen, complete the Present Complaint section of the case notes below.

SURNAME Hall		FIRST NAMES Kevin
AGE 32	SEX M	MARITAL STATUS M
OCCUPATION Lorry driver		
PRESENT COMPLAINT		

Now compare your notes with those made by the doctor. These are given in the Key on p. 105. Explain these sections in the notes.

1 SEX M

2 MARITAL STATUS M

3 3/12

4 a.m.

5 "dull, throbbing" Why are these words in quote marks (" ")?

6 c/o

Language focus 1

Note how the doctor starts the interview:

– *What's brought you along today?*

Other ways of starting an interview are:

– *What can I do for you?*
– *What seems to be the problem?*

Note how the doctor asks how long the problem has lasted.

– *How long have they been bothering you?*

Another way of asking about this is:

– *How long have you had them?*

Task 2

Study this short dialogue.

DOCTOR: Well, Mrs Black. *What's brought you along today?*
PATIENT: I've got a bad dose of flu. (1)
DOCTOR: *How long has it been bothering you?*
PATIENT: Two or three days. (2)

Practise this dialogue. Your partner should play the part of the patient. He or she can select replies from lists (1) and (2) below. Use all the ways of starting an interview and asking how long the problem has lasted.

(1)	*(2)*
a bad dose of flu	two or three days
terrible constipation	since Tuesday
swollen ankles	a fortnight
a pain in my stomach	for almost a month

Language focus 2

Note how the doctor asks where the problem is:

– *Which part of your head is affected?*

Other ways of finding this out are:

– *Where does it hurt?**
– *Where is it sore?**

Note how the doctor asks about the type of pain:

– *Can you describe the pain?*

Other ways of asking this are:

– *What's the pain like?*
– *What kind of pain is it?*

* *Hurt* is a verb. We use it like this: *My foot hurts.*
Sore is an adjective. We can say: *My foot is sore* or *I have a sore foot.*

Task 3

Practise finding out information like this. Work in the same way as in Task 2. Use all the methods given in Language focus 2 in your questioning.

DOCTOR: *Which part of your head (chest, back, etc.) is affected?*
PATIENT: Just here.
DOCTOR: *Can you describe the pain?*
PATIENT: It's a dull sort of ache. (1)

(1)
a dull sort of ache
a feeling of pressure
very sore, like a knife
a burning pain

Language focus 3

Note how the doctor asks if anything relieves the pain of headaches:
– *Is there anything that makes them better?**

Similarly he can ask:
– *Does anything make them worse?*

Doctors often ask if anything else affects the problem. For example:
– *What effect does food have?*
– *Does lying down help the pain?*

* *Better* means *improved* or *relieved*. It does not mean *cured*.

Task 4

Work with a partner. In each of these cases, ask your partner where the pain is. Then ask two other appropriate questions to help you reach a diagnosis. There is a diagram in the Key showing your partner where to indicate in each case. Use all the ways of questioning we have studied in this section. For example:

DOCTOR: *Where does it hurt?*
PATIENT: Right across here. (indicating the central chest area)
DOCTOR: *Can you describe the pain?*
PATIENT: It's like a heavy weight pressing on my chest.
DOCTOR: *Does anything make it better?*
PATIENT: If I stop for a bit, it goes away.

In this example, the patient's symptoms suggest angina.

Now try each of these four cases in the same way.

1 DOCTOR: ....

PATIENT: Here, just under my ribs. (1)

DOCTOR: ....

PATIENT: It gets worse and worse. Then it goes away.

DOCTOR: ....

PATIENT: Food makes it worse.

2 DOCTOR: ....

PATIENT: It's right here. (2)

DOCTOR: ....

PATIENT: It's a gnawing kind of pain.

DOCTOR: ....

PATIENT: Yes, if I eat, it gets better.

3 DOCTOR: ....

PATIENT: Down here. (3)

DOCTOR: ....

PATIENT: It's a sharp, stabbing pain. It's like a knife.

DOCTOR: ....

PATIENT: If I take a deep breath, or I cough, it's really sore.

4 DOCTOR: ....

PATIENT: Just here. (4)

DOCTOR: ....

PATIENT: My chest feels raw inside.

DOCTOR: ....

PATIENT: When I cough, it hurts most.

Task 5

Work in pairs. Student A should start.

A: Play the part of the doctor. Repeat Task 4 but add two or three more questions in each case to help you decide on a diagnosis. For instance, in the example where the patient's symptoms suggest angina, you could ask:
- *Does anything make it worse?*
- *How long does the pain last?*
- *Is there anything else you feel at the same time?*

B: Play the part of the patients. Use the replies in Task 4 and the extra information in the Key to help you.

These notes show the doctor's findings when he examined Mr Hall. Note the explanations given for the abbreviations used. What do the other ringed abbreviations stand for?

SURNAME	FIRST NAMES
AGE SEX	MARITAL STATUS
OCCUPATION	
PRESENT COMPLAINT	

O/E — ....
General Condition obese, 1.65m tall, 85 kg

ENT — Ear, Nose, Throat — wax ++ both sides

RS NAD — Nothing abnormal detected

CVS P — Pulse — 80/min reg. — regular — BP — .... — 180/120
HS — Heart sounds — normal

GIS — Gastro-intestinal system

GUS

CNS — .... — Fundi normal

IMMEDIATE PAST HISTORY

POINTS OF NOTE

INVESTIGATIONS
Urine -ve — .... — for sugar and albumen

DIAGNOSIS
? — .... — hypertension

MANAGEMENT
See 1/52 — ....

Task 7

Study this letter from a GP to a consultant. Write down the questions which a doctor might ask to obtain the information ringed in the letter. For example:

4 *How long did it last?*

8 *What was the cause of death?*

CLINICAL DETAILS

Date Oct 3rd 2004

Dear Dr Scott

I would be grateful for your opinion and advice with regard to

(Name) GREEN, Peter

URGENT
Please indicate in the box ☐

A brief outline of history, symptoms and signs and present therapy is given below:

This 42-year-old (salesman)[1] had a severe attack of (central chest pain)[2] (six months ago)[3] which (lasted 10 mins)[4] and was (relieved by rest.)[5] This has recurred several times (after exertion.)[6] His father (died aged 56)[7] of a (coronary thrombosis.)[8] Physical examination was normal and I refer him to you for further assessment in view of his age.

Diagnosis: angina

Thank you for seeing him.

Yours sincerely,

If transport required please state: ~~YES~~ NO

Stretcher/Sitting case

Sitting case – two man lift

Signature Mary Chapman

Task 8

The hospital consultant made these notes of her interview with Mr Green. Complete as many of the gaps as you can with the help of the letter on p. 10.

Then listen to the recording and complete the remaining gaps. Use the abbreviations you have studied in this unit.

SURNAME ....(1) FIRST NAMES Peter

AGE ....(2) SEX M MARITAL STATUS M

OCCUPATION ....(3)

PRESENT COMPLAINT
..............................(4) chest pain radiating to L arm. Started with severe attack c̄ dyspnoea. Pain lasted ....(5) relieved by rest. Has occurred since on exertion.

O/E
General Condition

ENT

RS Chest ....(6)

CVS ....(7) 70/min ....(8) 130/80
..............................(9) normal

GIS

GUS

CNS

IMMEDIATE PAST HISTORY

POINTS OF NOTE

INVESTIGATIONS

DIAGNOSIS

Study these case notes. What questions might the doctor have asked to obtain the information they contain?

a)

SURNAME James		FIRST NAMES Robert
AGE 48	SEX M	MARITAL STATUS S
OCCUPATION Builder		
PRESENT COMPLAINT c/o frontal headache 4/7 following cold. Worse in a.m. and when bending down. Also c/o being "off colour" and feverish.		
POINTS OF NOTE Analgesics c̄ some relief.		

b)

SURNAME Warner		FIRST NAMES Mary Elizabeth
AGE 34	SEX F	MARITAL STATUS D
OCCUPATION Teacher		
PRESENT COMPLAINT c/o episodic headaches many years, lasting 1–2 days every 3–4 months. Pain behind eyes c̄ nausea. "tightness" back of head. Depressed c̄ pain, interfering c̄ work.		

Task 10

Work in pairs and try to recreate the consultation. Student A should start.

A: Play the part of the patients. Use the case notes as prompts.

B: Play the part of the doctor. Find out what the patient is complaining of. Do not look at the case notes.

Section 3 Reading skills: Scanning a case history

Task 11

Read the following case history and find and underline this information about the patient as quickly as you can.

1 previous occupation

2 initial symptoms

3 initial diagnosis

4 condition immediately prior to admission

5 reason for emergency admission

6 duration of increased thirst and nocturia

7 father's cause of death

8 alcohol consumption

CASE HISTORY

Mr Wildgoose, a retired bus driver, was unwell and in bed with a cough and general malaise when he called in his general practitioner. A lower respiratory tract infection was diagnosed and erythromycin prescribed. Two days later, at a second home visit, he was found to be a little breathless and complaining that he felt worse. He was advised to drink plenty and to continue with his antibiotic. Another 2 days passed and the general practitioner returned to find the patient barely rousable and breathless at rest. Emergency admission to hospital was arranged on the grounds of 'severe chest infection'. On arrival in the ward, he was unable to give any history but it was ascertained from his wife that he had been confused and unable to get up for the previous 24h. He had been incontinent of urine on a few occasions during this time. He had been noted to have increased thirst and nocturia for the previous 2 weeks.

His past history included appendicectomy at age 11 years, cervical spondylosis 10 years ago, and hypertension for which he had been taking a thiazide diuretic for 3 years. His father had died at 62 years of myocardial infarction and his mother had had rheumatoid arthritis. His wife kept generally well but had also had a throat infection the previous week. Mr Wildgoose drank little alcohol and had stopped smoking 2 years previously.

Section 4 Case history: William Hudson

Task 12

In this section in each unit we will follow the medical history of William Hudson. In this extract he is visiting his new doctor for the first time. As you listen, complete the personal details and Present Complaint section of the case notes below.

SURNAME Hudson		FIRST NAMES William Henry
AGE	SEX	MARITAL STATUS
OCCUPATION		
PRESENT COMPLAINT		

Task 13

Work in pairs and try to recreate the consultation. Student A should start.

A: Play the part of William Hudson. Use the case notes to help you.

B: Play the part of the doctor. Find out what the patient is complaining of. Do not look at the case notes.

The case of William Hudson continues in Unit 2.

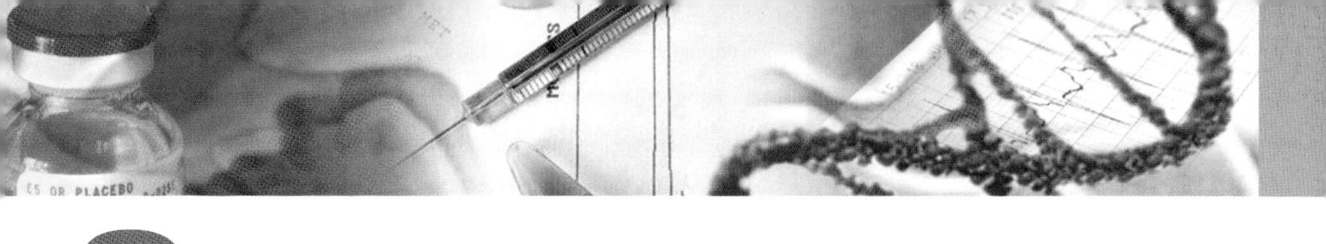

2 Taking a history 2

Section 1 Asking about systems

You will hear an extract from an interview between a doctor and her patient. The patient is a 50-year-old office worker who has complained of feeling tired, lacking energy and not being herself. As you listen, indicate whether the patient has a significant complaint or not by marking the appropriate column with a tick (✓) for each system.

System	*Complaint*	*No complaint*	*Order*
ENT			
RS			
CVS			
GIS			1
GUS			
CNS			
Psychiatric			

Listen again and number the order in which the information is obtained. The first one is marked for you.

Language focus 4

Note how the doctor asks about the systems:

- *Have you any trouble with* your stomach or bowels?
- *What's* your appetite *like*?
- *Any problems with* your waterworks?
- *What about* coughs or wheezing or shortness of breath?
- *Have you noticed* any weakness or tingling in your limbs?

Match each of the suspected problems in the first column with a suitable question from the second column. For example: 1c.

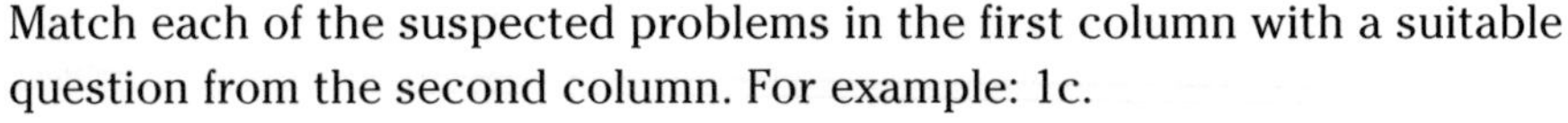

Suspected problem	*Question*
1 depression	a) Have you had any pain in your chest?
2 cardiac failure	b) Do you ever get wheezy?
3 asthma	c) What sort of mood have you been in recently?
4 prostate	d) Any problem with your waterworks?
5 coronary thrombosis	e) Have you ever coughed up blood?
6 cancer of the lung	f) Have you had any shortness of breath?

Work in pairs. Student A should start.

A: Play the part of the doctor. Ask questions about systems and specific problems for each of these cases. The patient has enough information to answer at least two key questions.

B: Play the part of the patients. Your information is given in the Key.

1 The patient is a man in late middle age. He has coughed up blood several times in the last few weeks.

2 The patient is an elderly man. He has been getting more and more constipated over the past few months.

3 The patient is a middle-aged woman. She gets pain in her stomach after meals.

4 The patient is a young woman. She has pain when she is passing urine.

5 The patient is a young man. He has a frontal headache.

When you have finished, look in the Key (p. 108) at the list of diagnoses. Select from the list the five diagnoses which match these cases.

Section 2 Asking about symptoms

Task 5

In this extract you will hear a physician interviewing a patient who has been admitted to hospital suffering from FUO (fever of unknown origin). The physician suspects TB. She has already asked about family history, etc. The following form is part of a FUO checklist. First listen and tick (✓) each point covered in the interview.

FEVER
- [1] duration
- [ ] frequency
- [ ] time
- [ ] chills
- [ ] sweats
- [ ] night sweats
- [ ] rigor

GENERAL SYMPTOMS
- [ ] malaise
- [ ] weakness
- [ ] myalgia
- [ ] wt loss
- [ ] drowsiness
- [ ] delirium
- [ ] anorexia
- [ ] vomiting
- [ ] photophobia

bleeding?
- [ ] nose
- [ ] skin
- [ ] urine

ACHES AND PAINS
- [ ] head
- [ ] teeth
- [ ] eyes
- [ ] abdomen
- [ ] chest
- [ ] neck
- [ ] loin
- [ ] back
- [ ] pubic
- [ ] muscle
- [ ] joints
- [ ] bone

SKIN
- [ ] rash
- [ ] pruritis
- [ ] bruising

CVS
- [ ] dyspnoea
- [ ] palpitations
- [ ] ht irregularity

GIS
- [ ] diarrhoea
- [ ] melaena

RESPIRATORY
- [ ] cough
- [ ] coryza
- [ ] sore throat
- [ ] dyspnoea
- [ ] pleuritic pain
- [ ] sputum
- [ ] haemoptysis

URINARY
- [ ] dysuria
- [ ] frequency
- [ ] strangury
- [ ] discolouration

NEUROLOGICAL
- [ ] vision
- [ ] photophobia
- [ ] blackouts
- [ ] diplopia

Task 6

Now listen again to indicate the order in which the points are covered by writing a number in the correct box. The first one is marked for you.

Language focus 5

Listen again to the FUO extract from Task 5. Note that the doctor uses rising intonation for these questions.

– *Any pain in your muscles?*
– *Have you lost any weight?*
– *Have you had a cough at all?*
– *Is there any blood in it?*
– *Have you had any pains in your chest?*

When we ask Yes/No questions like these, we normally use rising intonation. Note that the voice changes on the important word. For example:

– Any pain in your *muscles*?

Underline the important word in each of the questions above. Then listen again to see if you can hear the change on these words. Check your answers with the Key.

Study this extract from a case history.

The patient was a 59-year-old man, *head of a small engineering firm* (1), who *complained of central chest pain* (2) which occurred *on exertion* (3) and was *sometimes accompanied by sweating* (4). He *smoked 40 cigarettes a day* (5). The pain had *first appeared three months previously* (6) and was *becoming increasingly frequent* (7). He had noticed some *weight gain recently* (4 kg) (8) and also complained that his hair had become very dull and lifeless. He felt the cold much more than he used to. He *denied any palpitations* (9) or *ankle oedema* (10).

What questions might a doctor ask a patient to obtain the information in italics in the case history? Use the question types studied in Unit 1 and this unit. You may ask more than one question for each piece of information. For example:

1 What's your job?

2 What's brought you along today? Which part of your chest is affected?

When you have finished, put your questions in the most natural order for a consultation.

Work in pairs. Student A should start.

A: Play the part of the patient. Base your replies on the information given in the extract above.

B: Play the part of the doctor. Find out what the patient is complaining of.

Task 9

Here are some other questions which a doctor might ask a patient complaining of FUO. Which problems in the checklist in Task 5 do they refer to? Indicate on the form by writing the appropriate letter in the correct box.

Example: a) Have you any pain in passing water?

URINARY [a] dysuria

b) Do you suffer from double vision?

c) Any shortness of breath?

d) Does light bother you?

e) Are your stools black?

f) Do you have a cold?

Match each of the medical terms for common symptoms in the first column with a term which a patient would easily understand or might use, from the second column. For example: 1k.

Medical term	*Non-medical term*
1 paraesthesia	a) swelling, puffiness
2 productive cough	b) indigestion
3 anaesthesia	c) coughing up phlegm or spit
4 retrosternal chest pain	d) trouble holding your water
5 orthopnea	e) cramp in the leg muscles which comes and goes
6 stress incontinence	f) numbness
7 dysmenorrhoea	g) sleeplessness
8 dyspepsia	h) out of breath, out of puff, breathlessness
9 oedema	i) painful periods
10 intermittent claudication	j) pain behind the breast bone
11 insomnia	k) pins and needles
12 dyspnoea	l) shortness of breath when you lie down

Work in pairs. Student B should start.

A: Play the part of a patient. Use the information in the Key to help you.

B: Play the part of the doctor. Try to find out what the patient's problems are. Remember your patient will not understand medical terms. Remember also to use rising intonation for Yes/No questions. Record your findings in the Present Complaint section of the form below.

When you have finished, Student A should check the doctor's notes. Student B should compare his or her notes with the Key.

SURNAME Wilson		FIRST NAMES Peter
AGE 48	SEX M	MARITAL STATUS M
OCCUPATION Steelrope worker		
PRESENT COMPLAINT		

Task 12

This is part of a letter of referral from a doctor to a consultant concerning the same patient. Using the notes in the Key, complete this section of the letter. Use the appropriate medical terms.

Letter of referral (part 1)

Dear Dr MacPherson,

I'd be pleased to have your advice on the future management of this 48-year-old steelrope worker who gives a history of .... (1) on exertion of one year's duration and a .... (2) cough which he has had for some years.

During the last three weeks he has had three attacks of chest tightness and pain radiating into the upper right arm. The attacks have come on after exertion and have lasted several minutes. He has noticed ankle .... (3) increasing during the day and relieved by overnight rest. He also gives a month's history of .... (4) of the right leg relieved by rest. Last night he had an attack of acute .... (5) chest pain lasting 15 minutes, associated with extreme restlessness and a .... (6) spit.

He gives a history of good health but had childhood whooping cough and a wheezy bronchitis. He smokes an average of 20 to 30 cigarettes a day. His sister has a history of possible pulmonary tuberculosis and his father died of a heart attack at the age of 56.

Task 13

Study these findings on examination and details of the treatment given. Then complete the second part of the letter of referral.

SURNAME *Wilson*		FIRST NAMES *Peter*
AGE *48*	SEX *M*	MARITAL STATUS *M*
OCCUPATION *Steelrope worker*		

PRESENT COMPLAINT

Retrosternal chest pain last night radiating to neck and R arm. Duration 15 mins. Accompanied by restlessness. Diff. sleeping. Cough c̄ rusty spit. 1 yr SOBOE, productive cough some years, past $^{3}/_{52}$ tightness in chest x3, pain radiating to R arm, occurred on exertion, lasted mins.
Also $^{c}/_{o}$ puffy ankles in the evening, intermittent claudication R calf for $^{1}/_{12}$.

O/E

General Condition Short, barrel-chested, dyspnoea and peripheral cyanosis, early finger dubbing.

ENT

RS Poor resp. movt. Generalised hyper-resonance. Loss of liver dullness. Bilateral basal creps.

CVS P 84 reg. BP $^{140}/_{92}$ sitting. Oedema up to knees. Sacral oedema +. JVP ↑ Apex beat outside MCL in 6th L interspace. HS I, II faint. No peripheral pulses below popliteals.

GIS Liver palpable and tender. 2fb

GUS

CNS

MANAGEMENT

Rx frusemide 20 mg IV
morphine tartrate/cyclizine tartrate 15 mg IM

Letter of referral (part 2)

On examination, he is of .... (7) build with a barrel-shaped chest. He is .... (8) with some peripheral .... (9). There is also early finger .... (10). Pulse rate was 84, ... (11) in time and force. BP $^{140}/_{92}$ sitting. He has pitting .... (12) at the ankles to the level of the knee. There is also .... (13) sacral oedema. He has raised jugular .... (14) pressure.

On examination of his chest, he had poor respiratory movement, some hyper-resonance and loss of liver dullness. His apex beat was just outside the left-mid .... (15) line in the sixth left interspace. .... (16) sounds were closed but faint. He also had bilateral basal .... (17) while the liver seemed enlarged two finger breadths below the .... (18) costal margin and somewhat tender. The peripheral pulses in the lower limbs were impalpable below the popliteal arteries. He was given .... (19) frusemide, 20 mg, with good effect in relieving his breathlessness. Morphine tartrate/cyclizine tartrate, 15 mg was given .... (20).

Yours sincerely,

Task 14 Work in pairs. Student A should start.

A: Play the part of a trainee doctor. Ask about the findings on examination and treatment to date of Mr Wilson.

B: Play the part of the doctor who has examined Mr Wilson. Supply any information on Mr Wilson's examination and treatment using the notes given in Task 13.

You will hear a discussion between a general practitioner and a consultant. Complete the case notes below.

SURNAME		FIRST NAMES
AGE	SEX	MARITAL STATUS
OCCUPATION		
PRESENT COMPLAINT		
IMMEDIATE PAST HISTORY		

Task 16

This is a transcript of the conversation between the two doctors. Try to complete the consultant's questions. Then check your answers by listening to the recording.

GP: Hello, Jim. I wonder if you could see a patient for me?

CONSULTANT: Certainly, John. ....(1) the story?

GP: Well, it's a Mr Alan Jameson, a 53-year-old carpenter. He's been an infrequent attender in the past but he came to see me this morning complaining of *pain in his right leg and in his back* (a).

CONSULTANT: And ....(2) ....(3) this start?

GP: Well, *it came on about six weeks ago* (b) and it's become gradually more severe over the past couple of weeks.

CONSULTANT: ....(4) the pain localised?

GP: No, poorly. At first he thought he'd just pulled a muscle. But it's got so bad that he hasn't been able to do his work properly. It's also been getting to the stage where the *pain is waking him up at night* (c), it's been so severe, and he's *also noticed some tingling in his right foot* (d). *He's having difficulty in carrying on with his work* (e). He's *also lost three kilos* (f) and has become quite depressed.

CONSULTANT: ....(5) he ....(6) anything similar ....(7) the past?

GP: No, not exactly, but *he has suffered from intermittent pain in his back* (g). *Paracetamol gave some relief* (h) but didn't solve the problem completely.

CONSULTANT: Apart from ....(8), any ....(9) problems ....(10) health ....(11) the past?

GP: No, perfectly OK.

CONSULTANT: ....(12) you ....(13) anything else ....(14) examination?

GP: Yes, as well as the pain he has numbness in his toes on the right foot.

Task 17

Look at the information in italics in the transcript above. What questions might a doctor ask to obtain this kind of information from a patient? For example:

... *it came on about six weeks ago* (b)
Question: When did you first notice the pain?

Now try the other examples (a) to (h) in the same way. In which department do you think the consultant works?

Section 3 Reading skills: Noting information from a textbook

Task 18

Try to complete the table below which shows some of the key features of two medical problems. Then study the textbook extracts opposite to check your answers and to complete the table. This will help you make a differential diagnosis between the two problems.

	Angina	*Pericarditis*
Site		
Radiation		
Duration	a few minutes	persistent
Precipitating factors		
Relief of pain		
Accompanying symptoms and signs		

ANGINA PECTORIS

Angina pectoris is the term used to describe discomfort due to transient myocardial ischaemia and constitutes a clinical syndrome rather than a disease; it may occur whenever there is an imbalance between myocardial oxygen supply and demand.

FACTORS INFLUENCING MYOCARDIAL OXYGEN SUPPLY AND DEMAND

Oxygen demand
Cardiac work
- Heart rate
- Blood pressure
- Myocardial contractility

Oxygen supply
*Coronary blood flow**
- Duration of diastole
- Coronary perfusion pressure (aortic diastolic-right atrial diastolic pressure)
- Coronary vasomotor tone

Oxygenation
- Haemoglobin
- Oxygen saturation

*N.B. coronary blood flow is confined to diastole

Coronary atheroma is by far the most common cause but angina is also a feature of aortic valve disease, hypertrophic cardiomyopathy and some other forms of heart disease.

Clinical features
The history is by far the most important factor in making the diagnosis. Stable angina is characterised by left-sided or central chest pain that is precipitated by exertion and promptly relieved by rest.

Most patients describe a sense of oppression or tightness in the chest – 'like a band round the chest'; 'pain' may be denied. When describing angina the victim often closes a hand around the throat, puts a hand or clenched fist on the sternum, or places both hands across the lower chest. The term 'angina' is derived from the Greek word for strangulation and many patients report a 'choking' sensation. Breathlessness is sometimes a prominent feature.

The pain may radiate to the neck or jaw and is often accompanied by discomfort in the arms, particularly the left, the wrists and sometimes the hands; the patient may also describe a feeling of heaviness or uselessness in the arms. Occasionally the pain is epigastric or interscapular. Angina may occur at any of these places of reference without *chest* discomfort but a history of precipitation by effort, and relief by rest or sublingual nitrate, should still allow the condition to be recognised.

Symptoms tend to be worse after a meal, in the cold, and when walking uphill or into a strong wind. Some patients find that the pain comes when they start walking and that later it does not return despite greater effort ('start-up angina'). Some experience the pain when lying flat (decubitus angina), and some are awakened by it (nocturnal angina).

Angina may also occur capriciously as a result of coronary arterial spasm; occasionally this is accompanied by transient ST elevation on the ECG (Prinzmetal's or variant angina).

CLINICAL SITUATIONS PRECIPITATING ANGINA
- **Physical exertion**
- **Cold exposure**
- **Heavy meals**
- **Intense emotion**
- **Lying flat (decubitus angina)**
- **Vivid dreams (nocturnal angina)**

ACUTE PERICARDITIS

It is useful to classify the types of pericarditis both clinically and etiologically, since this disorder is by far the most common pathologic process involving the pericardium. Pain of a pericardial friction rub, electrocardiographic changes, and pericardial effusion with cardiac tamponade and paradoxic pulse are cardinal manifestations of many forms of acute pericarditis and will be considered prior to a discussion of the most common forms of the disorder.

Chest pain is an important but not invariable symptom in various forms of acute pericarditis; it is usually present in the acute infectious types and in many of the forms presumed to be related to hypersensitivity or autoimmunity. Pain is often absent in a slowly developing tuberculous postirradiation, neoplastic, or uremic pericarditis. The pain of pericarditis is often severe. It is characteristically retrosternal and left precordial referred to the back and the trapezius ridge. Often the pain is pleuritic consequent to accompanying pleural inflammation, i.e. sharp and aggravated by inspiration, coughing and changes in body position, but sometimes it is a steady, constrictive pain which radiates into either arm or both arms and resembles that of myocardial ischemia; therefore, confusion with myocardial infarction is common. Characteristically, however, the pericardial pain may be relieved by sitting up and leaning forward. The differentiation of acute myocardial infarction from acute pericarditis becomes even more perplexing when with acute pericarditis, the serum transaminase and creatine kinase levels rise, presumably because of concomitant involvement of the epicardium. However, these enzyme elevations, if they occur, are quite modest, given the extensive electrocardiographic ST-segment elevation in pericarditis.

The *pericardial friction rub* is the most important physical sign; it may have up to three components per cardiac cycle and is high-pitched, scratching, and grating; it can sometimes be elicited only when firm pressure with the diaphragm of the stethoscope is applied to the chest wall at the left lower sternal border. It is heard most frequently during expiration with the patient in the sitting position, but an independent pleural friction rub may be audible during inspiration with the patient leaning forward or in the left lateral decubitus position. The rub is often inconstant and transitory, and a loud to-and-fro leathery sound may disappear within a few hours, possibly to reappear the following day.

Moderate elevations of the MB fraction of creatine phosphokinase may occur and reflect accompanying epimyocarditis.

Section 4 Case history: William Hudson

Task 19

You will hear an extract from a consultation with Mr Hudson. The doctor has not seen him for seven years. He has just retired from the Post Office. As you listen, complete the Present Complaint section of the case notes below.

SURNAME Hudson		FIRST NAMES William Henry
AGE 65	SEX M	MARITAL STATUS
OCCUPATION Retired postmaster		
PRESENT COMPLAINT		

Task 20

Here is an edited version of the consultation. Complete the doctor's questions. Then check your answers with the recording and the Tapescript.

DOCTOR: Good afternoon, Mr Hudson. Just have a seat. I haven't seen you for a long time. ....(1) brought you here today?

PATIENT: Well, doctor, I've been having these headaches and I've lost a bit of weight.

DOCTOR: And how long ....(2) the headaches ....(3) bothering you?

PATIENT: Well, for quite a while now. The wife passed away four months ago. I've been feeling down since then.

DOCTOR: ....(4) part of your head is affected?

PATIENT: Just here, on the top. It feels like a heavy weight pressing down on me.

DOCTOR: ....(5) they affected your eyesight at all?

PATIENT: No, I wouldn't say so.

DOCTOR: They ....(6) made you ....(7) sick?

PATIENT: No.

DOCTOR: Now, you told me you've lost some weight. ....(8) your appetite ....(9) like?

PATIENT: I've been off my food.

DOCTOR: ....(10) about your bowels, ...(11) problems?

PATIENT: No, I'm quite all right.

DOCTOR: What ....(12) your waterworks?

PATIENT: Well, I've been having problems getting started and I have to get up two or three times at night.

DOCTOR: ....(13) this ....(14) on recently?

PATIENT: No, I've noticed it gradually over the past few months.

DOCTOR: ....(15) pain when you ....(16) water?

PATIENT: No.

DOCTOR: ....(17) you ....(18) any blood?

PATIENT: No.

Note how the actual consultation on the recording differs slightly from this version. What differences can you note? This consultation continues in Unit 3.

3 Examining a patient

Section 1 Giving instructions

Task 1

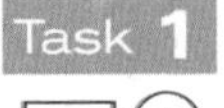

Mr Jameson (see Unit 2, p. 22) was examined by a neurologist. Study these drawings which show some of the movements examined. Predict the order in which the neurologist examined her patient by numbering the drawings. Drawing (e) shows the first movement examined.

Now listen to the extract from the neurologist's examination and check your predictions.

a) 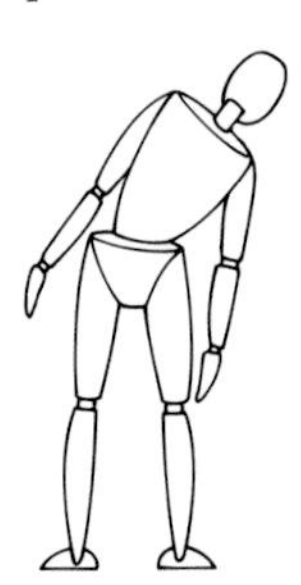

b) 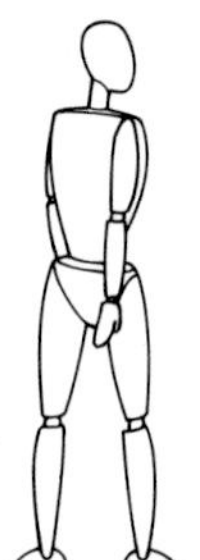

c) 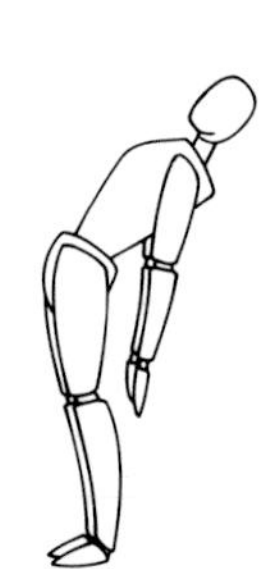

d) 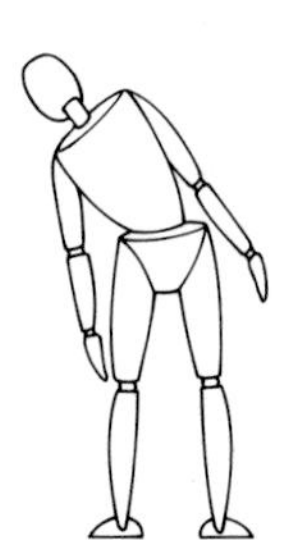

e) 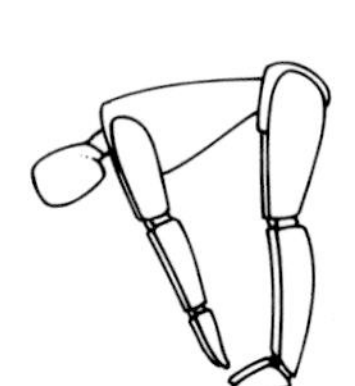

f) 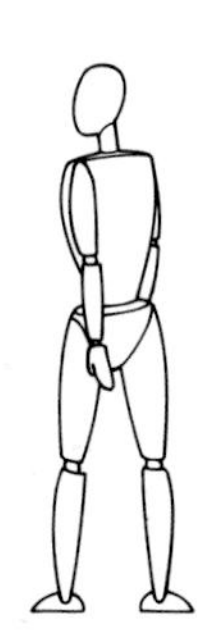

Language focus 6

Note how the doctor instructs the patient what to do:

– Now *I just want to see you* standing.
– *Could* you bend down as far as you can?
– *Keep* your knees and feet steady.

Instructions, especially to change position or remove clothing, are often made like this:

– *Would* you slip off your top things, please?
– Now *I would like you* to lean backwards.

The doctor often prepares the patient for the next part of the examination in this way:

– *I'm just going to* find out where the sore spot is.

Task 2

These drawings show a doctor testing a patient's reflexes. Predict the order in which the reflexes were tested by numbering them.

Now listen to the extract and check your predictions.

a)

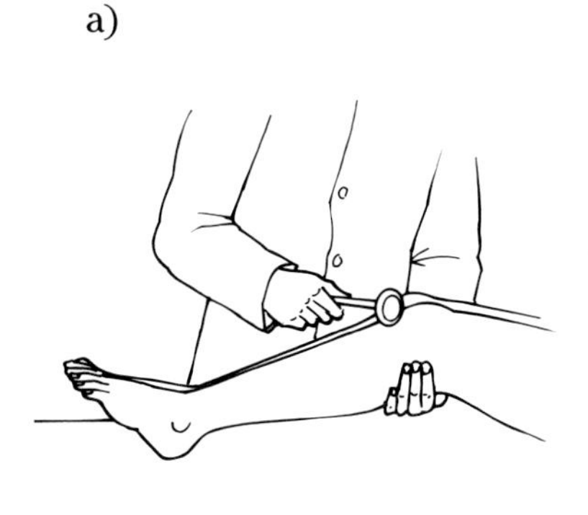

b)

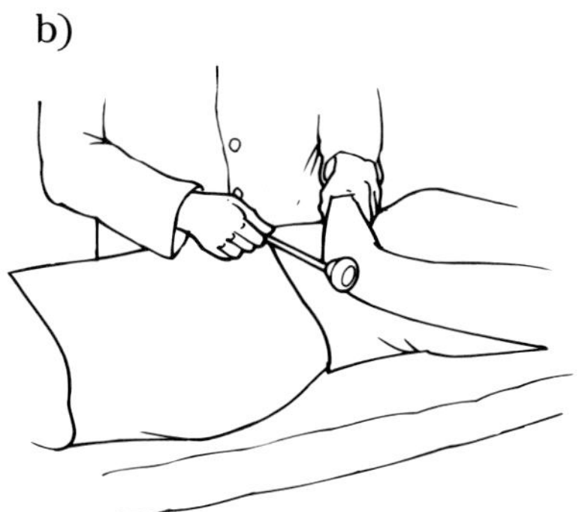

c)

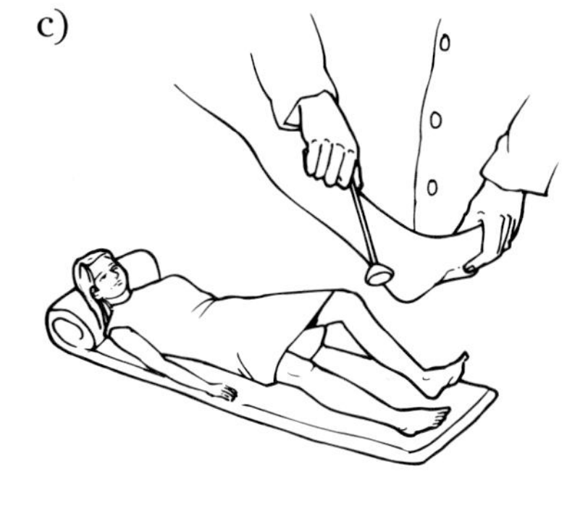

d)

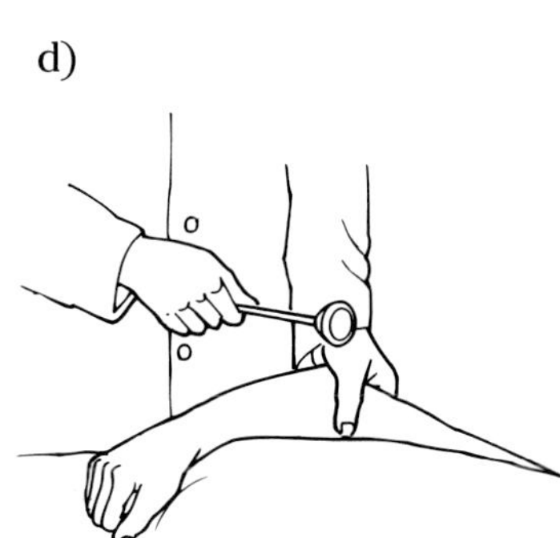

e)

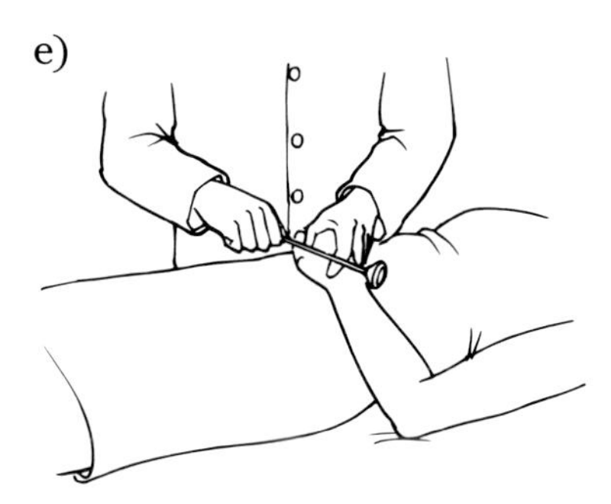

Task 3

Using the pictures in Task 2 to help you, write down what you would say to a patient to test these reflexes. When you have finished, compare your instructions and comments with the recording.

Task 4

Instruct a patient to take up the correct position, prepare him or her for these tests, and comment on each one.

1 Alternative method of eliciting the ankle jerk

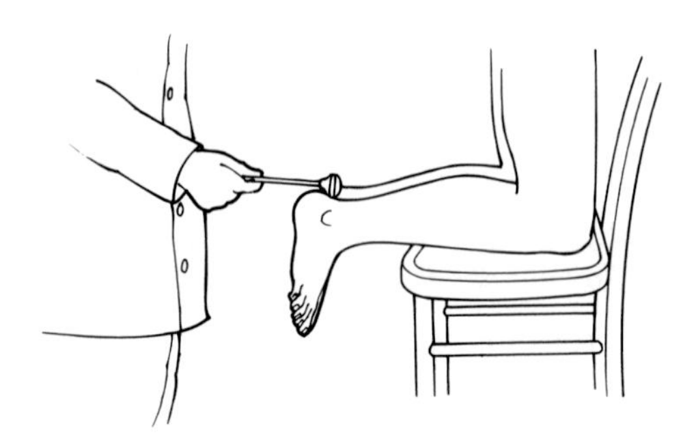

2 Reinforcement in eliciting the knee jerk

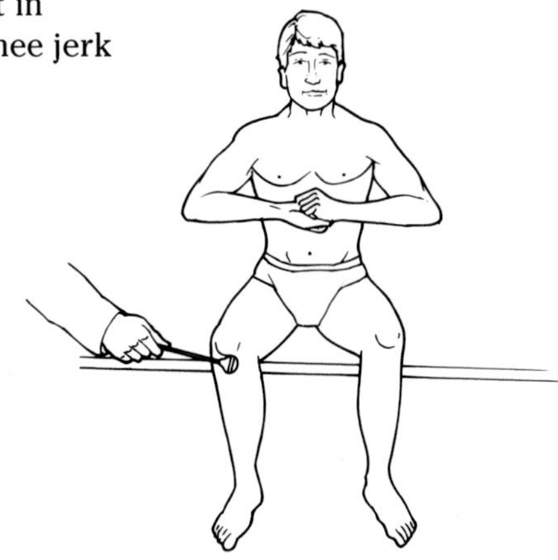

3 Eliciting the plantar reflex

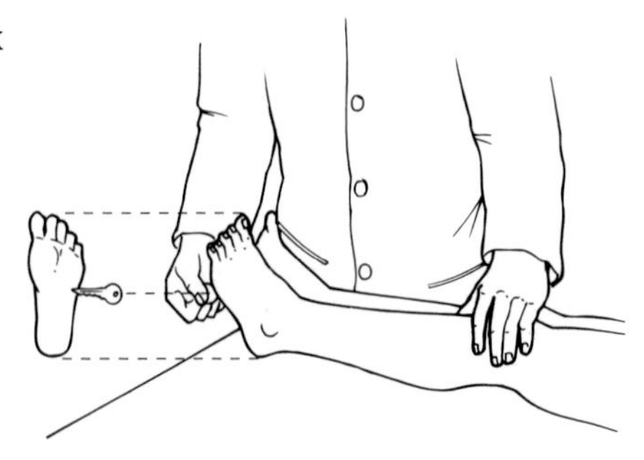

When you have finished, compare your instructions and comments with the recording.

Task 5

The neurologist carries out stretch tests on Mr Jameson for the sciatic and posterior tibial nerves and the femoral nerve. Complete the gaps in her instructions on the next page with the help of the drawings.

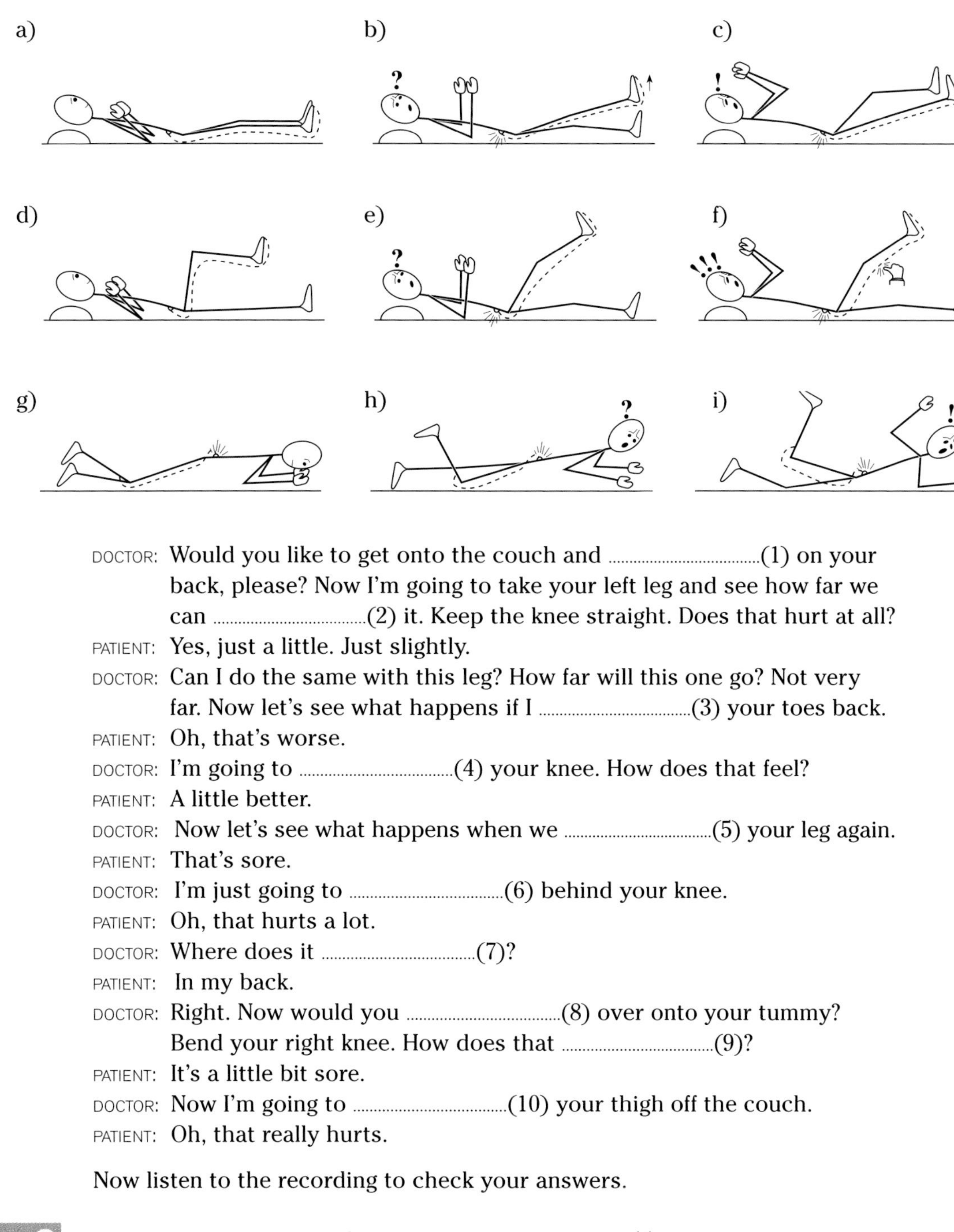

DOCTOR: Would you like to get onto the couch and ....(1) on your back, please? Now I'm going to take your left leg and see how far we can ....(2) it. Keep the knee straight. Does that hurt at all?

PATIENT: Yes, just a little. Just slightly.

DOCTOR: Can I do the same with this leg? How far will this one go? Not very far. Now let's see what happens if I ....(3) your toes back.

PATIENT: Oh, that's worse.

DOCTOR: I'm going to ....(4) your knee. How does that feel?

PATIENT: A little better.

DOCTOR: Now let's see what happens when we ....(5) your leg again.

PATIENT: That's sore.

DOCTOR: I'm just going to ....(6) behind your knee.

PATIENT: Oh, that hurts a lot.

DOCTOR: Where does it ....(7)?

PATIENT: In my back.

DOCTOR: Right. Now would you ....(8) over onto your tummy? Bend your right knee. How does that ....(9)?

PATIENT: It's a little bit sore.

DOCTOR: Now I'm going to ....(10) your thigh off the couch.

PATIENT: Oh, that really hurts.

Now listen to the recording to check your answers.

Task 6

A doctor has been called as an emergency to see a 55-year-old man at home with a history of high blood pressure who has collapsed with a sudden crushing central chest pain radiating to the back and legs. List what you would examine with such a patient.

Listen to the extract and note down what the doctor examined.

Compare your list with the examinations the doctor carried out.

Language focus 7

Listen to the recording again. Note how the doctor marks the end of each stage of the examination. Here are some of the ways he uses:

1 He pauses.

2 He uses expressions such as *OK, Fine, That's it.*

3 He uses falling intonation on these expressions.

Task 7

Turn back to Task 5. Using only the diagrams to help you, write down what you would say to the patient when making this examination. Then compare your answer with the Tapescript.

Section 2 Understanding forms

Task 8

Study this checklist for the first examination of a patient on attendance at an antenatal clinic. Some of these examinations are carried out as routine on subsequent visits. Mark them with a tick (✓) on the checklist.

THE FIRST EXAMINATION

1 Height ☐

2 Weight ☐

3 Auscultation of heart and lungs ☐

4 Examination of breasts and nipples ☐

5 Examination of urine ☐

6 Examination of pelvis ☐

7 Examination of legs ☐

8 Inspection of teeth ☐

9 Estimation of blood pressure ☐

10 Blood sample for blood group ☐

11 Blood sample for haemoglobin ☐

12 Blood sample for serological test for syphilis ☐

13 Blood sample for rubella antibodies ☐

14 Blood sample for HIV antibodies ☐

15 Examination of abdomen to assess size of uterus ☐

16 Examination of vagina and cervix ☐

Now study these extracts from an obstetrician's examination of a patient attending for her 32-week antenatal appointment. Match each extract to the numbered examinations on the checklist. For example:

a) Have you brought your urine sample? ....5....
b) Now would you like to sit up and I'll take your blood pressure? ....
c) Now I'll take a sample of blood to check your haemoglobin. ....
d) Have you noticed any swelling of your ankles? ... Let's have a quick look. ....
e) Now if you'd like to lie down on the couch, I'll take a look at the baby. I'll just measure to see what height it is. ....

Put the extracts on the previous page in the order in which you would prefer to carry out these examinations.

Work in pairs. Student A should start.

A: Play the part of the obstetrician. The card below shows the findings on examination of a patient attending for her 32-week appointment. Base your comments to the patient on these findings.

B: Play the part of the patient. You are attending for a 32-week appointment. Ask about anything the doctor says which you do not understand. Ask about anything on the card which you do not understand.

ANTENATAL No.

N.B. If there is anything on this card which you do not understand, do not hesitate to ask your Doctor or Midwife

		Pregnancy Test: Date Result	Ultrasound Scans	Date	BPD	Weeks		
L.M.P. ?22/3/03	Age 26	1. 4/5/03 +ve	1.	22/7/03	20	12-4	Surname	Wallace
E.D.D. 1. 3/2/04 2.	Parity 0 + 0	2.	2.				First Names	Mary
F.M.F.F.	Height 1.55		3.				Address	4 Waverley Park Wellington
	Blood Group O Rh + ve							

Date	Wks	Weight (kg)	Urine P	Urine S	BP	Fundus (cm) / Girth	Pres.	Level	FHH	Hb	Oed.	Problems, Investigations, Treatment etc (Please record all medicines)	Return Visit Date	Return Visit Place	G.P. Copy Sent
10/6/03	6	76			126/76							Discussed screening tests, diet, etc.			
22/7/03	12		Neg		125/90	N.P.				12.6					
19/8/03	16				120/80	16						AFP 16 wks. (Yes) No 16/8/03 Result normal			
7/10/03	22		Neg		110/80	22						FMF 3/52 ago			
11/11/03	26				120/80	28	Capt.		✔						
30/12/03	32		Neg		124/80	29	C	NE	✔	12.4		small for dates, ref. for scan			

Signature | Special features | **FOR OFFICE USE**

When you have completed your role-play, compare your version with the recorded consultation.

Section 3 Reading skills: Using a pharmacology reference

Task 11

Using the prescribing information which follows, choose the most appropriate antibiotic for these patients.

1 A 4-year-old-boy with meningitis due to pneumococcus. He is allergic to penicillin.
2 A 67-year-old man with a history of chronic bronchitis now suffering from pneumonia. The causative organism is resistant to tetracycline.
3 A 27-year-old woman with urinary tract infection in early pregnancy.
4 A 4-year-old girl with septic arthritis due to haemophilus influenzae.
5 An 18-year-old man with left leg amputation above the knee following a road traffic accident.
6 A 50-year-old woman with endocarditis caused by strep. viridans.
7 A 13-year-old girl with disfiguring acne.
8 An 8-year-old boy with tonsillitis due to ß-haemolytic streptococcus.
9 A 43-year-old dairyman with brucellosis.
10 A 4-year-old unimmunised sibling of a 2-year-old boy with whooping cough.

AMOXICILLIN
(Amoxycillin)

Indications: see under Ampicillin; also endocarditis prophylaxis (Table 2, section 5.1); and treatment (Table 1, section 5.1); anthrax (section 5.1.12); adjunct in listerial meningitis (Table 1, section 5.1); *Helicobacter pylori* eradication (section 1.3)

Cautions: see under Ampicillin

Contra-indications: see under Ampicillin

Side-effects: see under Ampicillin

Dose: *by mouth*, 250 mg every 8 hours, doubled in severe infections; CHILD up to 10 years, 125 mg every 8 hours, doubled in severe infections
Pneumonia, 0.5–1 g every 8 hours
Anthrax (treatment and post-exposure prophylaxis—see also section 5.1.12), 500 mg every 8 hours; CHILD body-weight under 20 kg, 80 mg/kg daily in 3 divided doses; body-weight over 20 kg, adult dose

Short-course oral therapy
Dental abscess, 3 g repeated after 8 hours
Urinary-tract infections, 3 g repeated after 10–12 hours
Otitis media, CHILD 3–10 years, 750 mg twice daily for 2 days

By intramuscular injection, 500 mg every 8 hours; CHILD, 50–100 mg/kg daily in divided doses

By intravenous injection or infusion, 500 mg every 8 hours increased to 1 g every 6 hours in severe infections; CHILD, 50–100 mg/kg daily in divided doses

ERYTHROMYCIN

Indications: alternative to penicillin in hypersensitive patients; campylobacter enteritis, pneumonia, legionnaires' disease, syphilis, non-gonococcal urethritis, chronic prostatitis, diphtheria and whooping cough prophylaxis; acne vulgaris and rosacea (section 13.6)

Cautions: hepatic and renal impairment; prolongation of QT interval (ventricular tachycardia reported); porphyria (section 9.8.2); pregnancy (not known to be harmful) and breast-feeding (only small amounts in milk); **interactions:** Appendix 1 (erythromycin and other macrolides)
ARRHYTHMIAS. Avoid concomitant administration with pimozide or terfenadine [other interactions, Appendix 1]

Side-effects: nausea, vomiting, abdominal discomfort, diarrhoea (antibiotic-associated colitis reported); urticaria, rashes and other allergic reactions; reversible hearing loss reported after large doses; cholestatic jaundice, cardiac effects (including chest pain and arrhythmias), myasthenia-like syndrome, Stevens-Johnson syndrome, and toxic epidermal necrolysis also reported

Dose: *by mouth*, ADULT and CHILD over 8 years, 250–500 mg every 6 hours *or* 0.5–1 g every 12 hours (see notes above); up to 4 g daily in severe infections; CHILD up to 2 years 125 mg every 6 hours, 2–8 years 250 mg every 6 hours, doses doubled for severe infections
Early syphilis, 500 mg 4 times daily for 14 days
Uncomplicated genital chlamydia, non-gonococcal urethritis, 500 mg twice daily for 14 days

By intravenous infusion, ADULT and CHILD severe infections, 50 mg/kg daily by continuous infusion *or* in divided doses every 6 hours; mild infections (oral treatment not possible), 25 mg/kg daily; NEONATE 30–45 mg/kg daily in 3 divided doses

PHENOXYMETHYLPENICILLIN
(Penicillin V)

Indications: tonsillitis, otitis media, erysipelas; rheumatic fever and pneumococcal infection prophylaxis (Table 2, section 5.1)

Cautions: see under Benzylpenicillin; **interactions:** Appendix 1 (penicillins)

Contra-indications: see under Benzylpenicillin

Side-effects: see under Benzylpenicillin

Dose: 500 mg every 6 hours increased up to 1 g every 6 hours in severe infections; CHILD, every 6 hours, up to 1 year 62.5 mg, 1–5 years 125 mg, 6–12 years 250 mg
NOTE. Phenoxymethylpenicillin doses in the BNF may differ from those in product literature

5.1.3 Tetracyclines

The tetracyclines are broad-spectrum antibiotics whose value has decreased owing to increasing bacterial resistance. They remain, however, the treatment of choice for infections caused by chlamydia (trachoma, psittacosis, salpingitis, urethritis, and lymphogranuloma venereum), rickettsia (including Q-fever), brucella (doxycycline with either streptomycin or rifampicin), and the spirochaete, *Borrelia burgdorferi* (Lyme disease—see section 5.1.1.3). They are also used in respiratory and genital mycoplasma infections, in acne, in destructive (refractory) periodontal disease, in exacerbations of chronic bronchitis (because of their activity against *Haemophilus influenzae*), and for leptospirosis in penicillin hypersensitivity (as an alternative to erythromycin).

Microbiologically, there is little to choose between the various tetracyclines, the only exception being **minocycline** which has a broader spectrum; it is active against *Neisseria meningitidis* and has been used for meningococcal prophylaxis but is no longer recommended because of side-effects including dizziness and vertigo (see section 5.1, table 2 for current recommendations). *Deteclo*® (a combination of tetracycline, chlortetracycline and demeclocycline) does not have any advantages over preparations containing a single tetracycline

CAUTIONS. Tetracyclines should be used with caution in patients with hepatic impairment (Appendix 2) or those receiving potentially hepatotoxic drugs. Tetracyclines may increase muscle weakness in patients with myasthenia gravis, and exacerbate systemic lupus erythematosus. Antacids, and aluminium, calcium, iron, magnesium and zinc salts decrease the absorption of tetracyclines; milk also reduces the absorption of demeclocycline, oxytetracycline, and tetracycline. Other **interactions:** Appendix 1 (tetracyclines).

CONTRA-INDICATIONS. Deposition of tetracyclines in growing bone and teeth (by binding to calcium) causes staining and occasionally dental hypoplasia, and they should **not** be given to children under 12 years, or to pregnant or breast-feeding women (Appendixes 4 and 5). However, doxycycline may be used in children for treatment and post-exposure prophylaxis of anthrax when an alternative antibacterial cannot be given [unlicensed indication]. With the exception of **doxycycline** and **minocycline**, the tetracyclines may exacerbate renal failure and should **not** be given to patients with kidney disease (Appendix 3).

SIDE-EFFECTS. Side-effects of the tetracyclines include nausea, vomiting, diarrhoea (antibiotic-associated coltis reported occasionally), dysphagia, and oesophageal irritation. Other rare side-effects include hepatotoxicity, blood dyscrasias, photosensitivity (particularly with demeclocycline), and hypersensitivity reactions (including rash, exfoliative dermatitis, urticaria, angioedema, anaphylaxis, pericarditis). Headache and visual disturbances may indicate benign intracranial hypertension (discontinue treatment); bulging fontanelles have been reported in infants.

TETRACYCLINE

Indications: see notes above; acne vulgaris, rosacea (section 13.6)

Cautions: see notes above

Contra-indications: see notes above

Side-effects: see notes above; also reported, pancreatitis, acute renal failure, skin discoloration

Dose: *by mouth*, 250 mg every 6 hours, increased in severe infections to 500 mg every 6–8 hours

Acne, see section 13.6.2

Non-gonococcal urethritis, 500 mg every 6 hours for 7–14 days (21 days if failure or relapse after first course)

COUNSELLING. Tablets should be swallowed whole with plenty of fluid while sitting or standing

CEFUROXIME

Indications: see under Cefaclor; surgical prophylaxis; more active against *Haemophilus influenzae* and *Neisseria gonorrhoeae*; Lyme disease

Cautions: see under Cefaclor

Contra-indications: see under Cefaclor

Side-effects: see under Cefaclor

Dose: *by mouth* (as cefuroxime axetil), 250 mg twice daily in most infections including mild to moderate lower respiratory-tract infections (e.g. bronchitis); doubled for more severe lower respiratory-tract infections or if pneumonia suspected

Urinary-tract infection, 125 mg twice daily, doubled in pyelonephritis

Gonorrhoea, 1 g as a single dose

CHILD over 3 months, 125 mg twice daily, if necessary doubled in child over 2 years with otitis media

Lyme disease, ADULT and CHILD over 12 years, 500 mg twice daily for 20 days

By intramuscular injection or intravenous injection or infusion, 750 mg every 6–8 hours; 1.5 g every 6–8 hours in severe infections; single doses over 750 mg intravenous route only

CHILD usual dose 60 mg/kg daily (range 30–100 mg/kg daily) in 3–4 divided doses (2–3 divided doses in neonates)

Gonorrhoea, 1.5 g as a single dose *by intramuscular injection* (divided between 2 sites)

Surgical prophylaxis, 1.5 g *by intravenous injection* at induction; up to 3 further doses of 750 mg may be given *by intramuscular or intravenous* injection every 8 hours for high-risk procedures

Meningitis, 3 g intravenously every 8 hours; CHILD, 200–240 mg/kg daily (in 3–4 divided doses) reduced to 100 mg/kg daily after 3 days or on clinical improvement; NEONATE, 100 mg/kg daily reduced to 50 mg/kg daily

GENTAMICIN

Indications: septicaemia and neonatal sepsis; meningitis and other CNS infections; biliary-tract infection, acute pyelonephritis or prostatitis, endocarditis (see notes above); pneumonia in hospital patients, adjunct in listerial meningitis (Table 1, section 5.1)

Cautions: pregnancy (Appendix 4), renal impairment, infants and elderly (adjust dose and monitor renal, auditory and vestibular function together with serum gentamicin concentrations); avoid prolonged use; conditions characterised by muscular weakness; significant obesity (monitor serum-gentamicin concentration closely and possibly reduce dose); see also notes above; **interactions:** Appendix 1 (aminoglycosides)

Contra-indications: myasthenia gravis

Side-effects: vestibular and auditory damage, nephrotoxicity; rarely, hypomagnesaemia on prolonged therapy, antibiotic-associated colitis; also reported, nausea, vomiting, rash; see also notes above

Dose: *by intramuscular or by slow intravenous injection* over at least 3 minutes *or by intravenous infusion*, 3–5 mg/kg daily (in divided doses every 8 hours), see also notes above

CHILD up to 2 weeks, 3 mg/kg every 12 hours; 2 weeks–12 years, 2 mg/kg every 8 hours

Streptococcal or enterococcal endocarditis in combination with other drugs, 80 mg twice daily

Endocarditis prophylaxis, Table 2, section 5.1

By intrathecal injection, seek specialist advice, 1 mg daily (increased if necessary to 5 mg daily)

NOTE. One-hour ('peak') serum concentration should be 5–10 mg/litre (3–5 mg/litre for streptococcal or enterococcal endocarditis); pre-dose ('trough') concentration should be less than 2 mg/litre (less than 1 mg/litre for streptococcal or enterococcal endocarditis)

BENZYLPENICILLIN

(Penicillin G)

Indications: throat infections, otitis media, streptococcal endocarditis, meningococcal disease, pneumonia (Table 1, section 5.1); anthrax; prophylaxis in limb amputation (Table 2, section 5.1)

Cautions: history of allergy; renal impairment (Appendix 3); **interactions:** Appendix 1 (penicillins)

Contra-indications: penicillin hypersensitivity

Side-effects: hypersensitivity reactions including urticaria, fever, joint pains, rashes, angioedema, anaphylaxis, serum sickness-like reactions, haemolytic anaemia and interstitial nephritis; neutropenia, thrombocytopenia, coagulation disorders and central nervous system toxicity including convulsions reported (especially with high doses or in severe renal impairment); diarrhoea and antibiotic-associated colitis

Dose: *by intramuscular or by slow intravenous injection or by infusion*, 2.4–4.8 g daily in 4 divided doses, increased if necessary in more serious infections (see also below); PREMATURE INFANT and NEONATE, 50 mg/kg daily in 2 divided doses; INFANT 1–4 weeks, 75 mg/kg daily in 3 divided doses; CHILD 1 month–12 years, 100 mg/kg daily in 4 divided doses (higher doses may be required, see also below)

Bacterial endocarditis, *by slow intravenous injection or by infusion*, 7.2 g daily in 6 divided doses

Anthrax (in combination with other antibacterials, see also section 5.1.12), *by slow intravenous injection* or *by infusion*, 2.4 g every 4 hours; CHILD 150 mg/kg daily in 4 divided doses

Meningococcal disease, *by slow intravenous injection or by infusion*, 2.4 g every 4 hours; PREMATURE INFANT and NEONATE, 100 mg/kg daily in 2 divided doses; INFANT 1–4 weeks, 150 mg/kg daily in 3 divided doses; CHILD 1 month–12 years, 180–300 mg/kg daily in 4–6 divided doses

Important. If bacterial meningitis and especially if meningococcal disease is suspected general practitioners are advised to give a single injection of benzylpenicillin by intravenous injection (or by intramuscular injection) before transferring the patient urgently to hospital. Suitable doses are: ADULT 1.2 g; INFANT 300 mg; CHILD 1–9 years 600 mg, 10 years and over as for adult. In **penicillin allergy**, cefotaxime (section 5.1.2) may be an alternative; chloramphenicol may be used if there is a history of anaphylaxis to penicillins

By intrathecal injection, **not** recommended

NOTE. Benzylpenicillin doses in BNF may differ from those in product literature

CEFOTAXIME

Indications: see under Cefaclor; gonorrhoea (section 5.1, table 1); surgical prophylaxis; Haemophilus epiglottitis and meningitis (section 5.1, table 1); see also notes above

Cautions: see under Cefaclor

Contra-indications: see under Cefaclor

Side-effects: see under Cefaclor; rarely arrhythmias following rapid injection reported

Dose: *by intramuscular or intravenous injection or by intravenous infusion*, 1 g every 12 hours increased in severe infections (e.g. meningitis) to 8 g daily in 4 divided doses; higher doses (up to 12 g daily in 3–4 divided doses) may be required; NEONATE 50 mg/kg daily in 2–4 divided doses increased to 150–200 mg/kg daily in severe infections; CHILD 100–150 mg/kg daily in 2–4 divided doses increased up to 200 mg/kg daily in very severe infections

Gonorrhoea, 500 mg as a single dose

Important. If bacterial meningitis and especially if meningococcal disease is suspected the patient should be transferred urgently to hospital. If benzylpenicillin cannot be given (e.g. because of an allergy), a single dose of cefotaxime may be given (if available) before urgent transfer to hospital. Suitable doses of cefotaxime by intravenous injection (or by intramuscular injection) are ADULT and CHILD over 12 years 1 g; CHILD under 12 years 50 mg/kg; chloramphenicol (section 5.1.7) may be used if there is a history of anaphylaxis to penicillins or cephalosporins

Section 4 Case history: William Hudson

Study these case notes from Mr Hudson's consultation, part of which you studied in Unit 2, Section 4. Try to work out the meanings of the circled abbreviations. Refer to Appendix 2 for help.

SURNAME Hudson	FIRST NAMES William Henry
AGE 65 SEX M	MARITAL STATUS W
OCCUPATION Retired postmaster	

PRESENT COMPLAINT
Headaches for 4 mths. Wt loss. Headaches feel "like a heavy weight".
No nausea or visual symptoms.
No appetite.
Diff. starting to PU. Nocturia x3.

O/E
General Condition

ENT

RS chest clear

CVS P $^{110}/_{min}$ irreg. ? AF BP $^{160}/_{105}$ HS I,II

GIS abdo. NAD

GUS p.r. prostate moderately enlarged

CNS NAD

IMMEDIATE PAST HISTORY

POINTS OF NOTE
Wife died $^{4}/_{12}$ ago of Ca. ovary.

INVESTIGATIONS

The case notes record the doctor's findings on examination. Write down what you would say to Mr Hudson when carrying out this examination. Then listen to the recording to compare your answer.

You decide to refer Mr Hudson for further treatment. The surgeon is Mr Fielding. Write a letter to him outlining Mr Hudson's problems. Use the form below. When you have finished, compare your version with the Key. The case of Mr Hudson continues in Unit 4.

Hospital use Only	Clinic	Day Date	Time	Hospital No.	GP112

Ambulance Required Sitting/Stretcher Yes No

REQUEST FOR OUT-PATIENT CONSULTATION

Hospital .... Date ....

Urgent Appointment Required Yes No

PARTICULARS OF PATIENT IN BLOCK LETTERS PLEASE

Please arrange for this patient to attend the .... clinic of Dr/Mr ....

Patient's Surname .... Maiden Surname ....

First Names .... Single/Married/Widowed/Other

Address .... Date of Birth ....

.... Patient's Occupation ....

Postal Code .... Telephone Number ....

Has the patient attended hospital before: YES/NO? If "YES" please state:

Name of Hospital ....

Year of Attendance .... Hospital No. ....

If the patient's name and/or address has/have changed since then please give details:

....

....

....

....

....

Name, Address and Telephone Number of MEDICAL/DENTAL PRACTITIONER

Please use rubber stamp

I would be grateful for your opinion and advice on the above named patient. A brief outline of history, symptoms and signs is given below:

Diagnosis/provisional diagnosis: ....

Present drug treatment and potential special hazards: ....

Relevant X-rays available from: .... No. (if known) ....

Signature ....

4 Special examinations

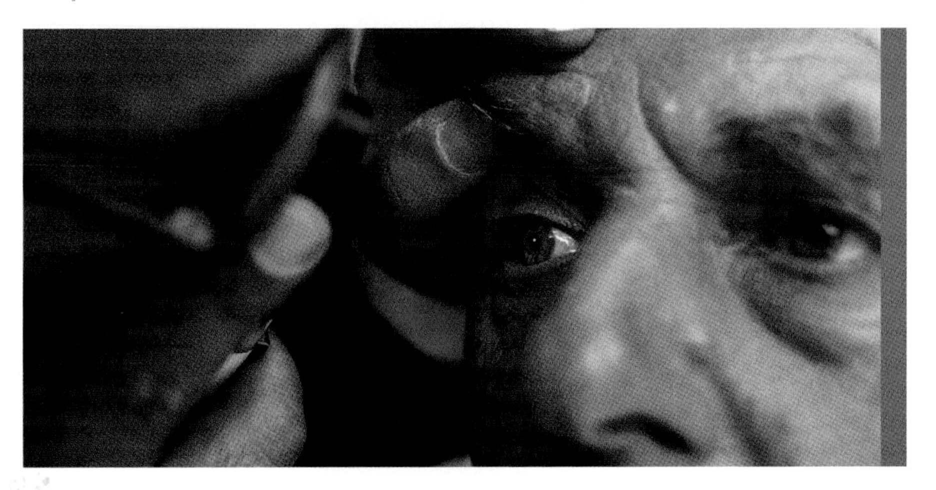

Section 1 Instructing, explaining and reassuring

Task 1

You will hear an interview between a hospital consultant, Mr Davidson, and a patient, Mr Priestly. As you listen, complete the case notes and decide which department the patient has been referred to.

SURNAME		FIRST NAMES John
AGE 58	SEX M	MARITAL STATUS M
OCCUPATION		
PRESENT COMPLAINT		

Task 2

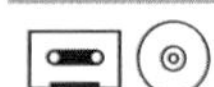

Now listen again to complete the doctor's questions.

1 Can you see any letters at ....(a) ?
2 Well, with the right eye, ...(b) you see ....(c) ?
3 Now does ....(d) make ....(e) difference?
4 What about ....(f) one? Does ....(g) have any effect?

What do you think (d) and (f) refer to?

Task 3

Think about the intonation of the completed questions in Task 2. Mark the words where you expect the speaker's voice to go up or down.

Now listen to the recording to check your answers.

> **Language focus 8**
>
> Note how the doctor starts the examination:
>
> – *I'd just like to ...*
> – *Could you just ... for me?*
>
> Note how the doctor indicates the examination is finished:
>
> – *Right, thank you very much indeed.*

Task 4

You want to examine a patient. Match the examinations in the first column with the instructions in the second column. Then practise with a partner what you would say to a patient when carrying out these examinations. Rephrase the instructions according to what you have studied in this unit and in Unit 3. For example:

1–d I'd just like to examine your throat. Could you please open your mouth as wide as you can?

Examinations	*Instructions*
1 the throat	a) Remove your sock and shoe.
2 the ears	b) Remove your top clothing.
3 the chest	c) Turn your head this way.
4 the back	d) Open your mouth.
5 the foot	e) Tilt your head back.
6 the nasal passage	f) Stand up.

Task 5

What do you think the doctor is examining by giving each of these instructions?

1 I want you to push as hard as you can against my hand.
2 Breathe in as far as you can. Now out as far as you can.
3 Say 99. Now whisper it.
4 Could you fix your eyes on the tip of my pen and keep your eyes on it?
5 I want you to keep this under your tongue until I remove it.
6 Would you roll over on your left side and bend your knees up? This may be a bit uncomfortable.
7 I want to see you take your right heel and run it down the front of your left leg.
8 Put out your tongue. Say Aah.

Task 6

Work in pairs and look back at Task 1. Student A should start.

A: Play the part of Mr Davidson.

1 Greet the patient.
2 Indicate that you have had a letter of referral.
3 Ask about the duration of the problem.
4 Ask about the patient's occupation.
5 Ask about the effect on his occupation.
6 Indicate that you would like to examine him.
7 Ask him to read the chart.
8 Ask about the right eye.
9 You change the lens – does it make any difference?
10 You try another one.
11 Indicate that the examination is over.

B: Play the part of Mr Priestly. Use the case notes as prompts.

Task 7

You will hear an extract from an examination. As you listen, tick off the systems examined.

System	*Examined*
ENT	
RS	
CVS	
GIS	
GUS	
CNS	
Others (specify)	

What kind of examination is this?
How old do you think the patient is?
How do you know?

Language focus 9

Note how the doctor carefully reassures the patient by explaining what she is going to do and indicating that everything is all right:

– *Can I have a look at you to find out where your bad cough is coming from? ... That's fine.*

Try to complete the doctor's explanations and expressions of reassurance by adding one word in each gap.

Now listen to the extract again and check your answers.

1 Now I'm ....(a) to put this thing on your chest.

2 It's ....(b) a stethoscope.

3 It ....(c) be a bit cold.

4 OK? First ....(d) all, I listen ....(e) your front and ....(f) your back.

5 Well ....(g), you didn't move at all.

6 Now I'd ....(h) to see your tummy, ...(i) will you lie on the bed for a minute?

7 Now while ....(j) lying there, ...(k) feel your neck and under your arms.

8 Are you ....(l)?

9 ....(m) the top of your legs.

10 That's ....(n) very quick, ...(o) it?

Listen again. Try to note the intonation of the question forms.

Look back to Task 4. How would you rephrase the instructions for a 4-year-old? When you have finished, look at the Key and listen to the recording.

Section 2 Rephrasing, encouraging and prompting

The form below is used to measure mental impairment. Discuss with a partner:

- in what order you might ask these questions
- in what form you might ask them

ISAACS-WALKEY MENTAL IMPAIRMENT MEASUREMENT

Date of test / /

Ask the patient the following questions.
Score 1 for a correct answer, 0 for an error.

	Score
1 What is the name of this place?	....
2 What day of the week is it today?	....
3 What month is it?	....
4 What year is it?	....
5 What age are you? (allow ±1 year error)	....
6 In what year were you born?	....
7 In what month is your birthday?	....
8 What time is it? (allow ±1 hour error)	....
9 How long have you been here? (allow 25% error)	....
Total score	....

Significance of score

8 or 9	No significant impairment
5 to 7	Moderate impairment
1 to 4	Severe impairment
0	Complete failure

Signature of examiner ....

You will hear an interview between a doctor and a patient he has known for years. As you listen, number the questions above in the order they are asked. Compare the order with your predictions.

Complete Task 12 before you check your answers in the Key.

Task 12 Study the information about the patient given below. Then listen to the interview again with the purpose of giving the patient a score.

SURNAME Walters		FIRST NAMES John Edward
AGE 83	SEX M	MARITAL STATUS W
OCCUPATION Retired millworker		

Date of test: Thursday 27 February 1997
Patient's DOB: 17 April 1913

How does your score compare with that given by your partner and in the Key?

Language focus 10

Note how the doctor uses a rephrasing technique to encourage the patient and give him time to answer. For example:

Question 9: Have you been here long?
In this house, have you been here long?
How long have you been living in the High Street?

Note also that the rephrased question is often preceded by an expression like *Do you remember ...?* For example:
– *Do you remember where this is? Where is this place?*

Task 13 Predict the missing words in these extracts. Several words are required in most of the gaps. Then listen again to the interview to check your predictions. Try to match the rephrasings with the corresponding test questions. Example (a) is done for you.

a) Question ...6... : Do you remember when you were born?
What ....(1) ?
Can you ....(2) ?
b) Question .... : Do you remember what time of the month?
What ....(3) ?
c) Question .... : How old will you be now ....(4) ?
d) Question .... : What year is it this year? Do you ....(5) ?
e) Question .... : Fine, and what month are we in?
Well, ...(6) ?
f) Question .... : Do you remember what day of the week it is?
Or do the ....(7) now that you're ....(8) ?

Think about the intonation of the completed questions in Task 13. Mark the words where you expect the speaker's voice to go up or down.

Now listen to the recording to check your answers.

Look back at the test form in Task 10. Think of at least two ways of rephrasing each question.

Mr Jameson (see Unit 3, p. 28) was referred to a neurologist for examination. During the examination the neurologist touches Mr Jameson with:

a) a needle

b) a piece of cotton wool

c) hot and cold tubes

d) a vibrating fork

Listen to Parts 1 to 4 of the examination and number the steps in the order that the neurologist carries them out.

Language focus 11

Note how the neurologist explains what she is going to do in Part 1 of the examination:

- *I now want to ...*
- *I'm going to ...*
- *I'll ...*

Listen to Part 1 of the interview to complete these explanations. Then listen to Parts 2, 3 and 4 to note:

a) How the doctor instructs the patient.

b) How the doctor marks the stages of her examination.

To instruct the patient, she uses:

- *I want you to ...*

To mark the stages of her examination, she says:

- *Now I'm going to try something ...*
- *Next I'm going to test you ...*

Using the expressions studied in Language focus 11, explain to Mr Jameson each stage of the examination and instruct him.

Task 18

The neurologist then examines Mr Jameson's leg pulses. The sequence of examination is as follows:

1 the groin
2 behind the knee
3 behind the ankle bone
4 the top of the foot
5 the other leg

Write what you would say to Mr Jameson. Then listen to Part 5 of the examination to compare.

Task 19

Work in pairs. Choose a specialist examination in your own field. Together decide how you can explain to the patient each stage of the examination and how you would instruct the patient. Then find a new partner to play the patient.

Section 3 Reading skills: Reading articles 1

Task 20

Here are the headings that are commonly used in articles from American journals. Number them in the order that you would expect them to feature.

References
Summary
Comment
Materials and methods
Authors
Editor's note
Title
Results
Introduction

Task 21

Here are some brief extracts from an article that featured in the *Archives of Pediatric and Adolescent Medicine*. Try to match them to the headings given in Task 20. What features of the text helped you to identify the parts?

Now put the headings in the order that you would expect to find them.

a) *Kathi J. Kemper, MD, MPH; Paul L. McCarthy, MD; Domenic V. Cicchetti, PhD*

c)

1. Standards of Reporting Trials Group. A proposal for structured reporting of randomized controlled trials. *JAMA*. 1994; 272: 1926–1931.
2. Working Group on Recommendations for Reporting Clinical Trials in the Biomedical Literature. Call for comments on a proposal to improve reporting of clinical trials in the biomedical literature. *Ann Intern Med*. 1994; 121: 894–895.
3. Haynes RB, Mulrow CD, Huth EJ, Altman DG, Gardner MJ. More informative abstracts revisited. *Ann Intern Med*. 1990; 113: 69–76.
4. Purpose and procedure. *ACP J Club*. 1991; 115 (suppl 2): A-13–A-14.

b)

Abstract scoring and selection remained constant throughout the study years. All abstracts were rated anonymously, ie authors' names and institutions were omitted. All abstracts were rated from 1 to 5, with 1 indicating unsuitable for presentation; 2, consider only if necessary; 3, borderline; 4, good; 5, a "must". The ratings for each abstract were averaged. Abstracts were sorted by rank, with the highest average scores at the top. The top abstracts were selected for platform (oral) presentation. As space allowed, the next highest-scoring abstracts were selected for poster presentation.

Between 1990 and 1991, the number of reviewers per abstract was reduced from 11 to six. In 1995, the pool of reviewers was expanded to include the chairpersons of two SIGs—ER and BEH—and 10 regional chairpersons (RCs). Abstracts were divided into three categories: ER, BEH, and GP. The ER abstracts were reviewed by the chairperson of the ER SIG, two RCs, and one member of the BOD. The BEH abstracts were reviewed by the chairperson of the BEH SIG, two RCs, and two members of the BOD. The GP abstracts were reviewed by five members of the BOD and six RCs, so every abstract was reviewed by at least five raters. Specific assignments were made randomly by administrative staff at the APA office.

d)

The number of abstracts submitted and selected for presentation in 1990, 1991, 1993, and 1995 are given in **Table 1**. Data from 1991 and 1993 are included for comparison.

The number of abstracts submitted for consideration for presentation at the annual APA meeting increased steadily between 1990 and 1995. The increased capacity for poster presentations each year since 1990 increased the overall acceptance rate from 42% in 1990, when 14 posters were presented, to 62% in 1995, when 182 posters were presented. The number of oral presentations remained constant at about 90 per year since the late 1980s.

Of all abstracts submitted to APA in 1995, 246 were reviewed by the GP committee (11 reviewers), 118 were reviewed by the ER committee (four reviewers), and 43 were reviewed by the BEH committee (five reviewers). There were no reported logistical problems as a result of increasing the number and variety of reviewers. All reviews were returned within 10 days.

e)

> A few cannot agree. Add more, and they also cannot agree. If not reliable, at least they are consistent. Perhaps this should be entitled "Raters of the Lost Art".
>
> *Catherine D. DeAngelis, MD*

f)

> These results are consistent with previous studies of the peer review process indicating that after correcting for chance, interrater agreement is poor. Without specific criteria and training for reviewers, interrater agreement is only slightly better than chance. This is also true for evaluating funding proposals[23] and in clinical medicine.[24] Interrater agreement on the quality of patient care often shows κ values less than 0.40.[25]

g)

> PEER REVIEW is a cornerstone of the modern scientific process. It is the means by which grant applications are selected for funding, experiments involving human subjects are approved, manuscripts are selected for publication, and abstracts are selected for presentation at scientific meetings. Research presentations help disseminate new knowledge and may improve patient care, health services, and health education. Through abstract presentations, new researchers are introduced to the academic community and career development is enhanced. Failure to be accepted for presentation often has damaging effects on junior investigators' self-esteem and interest in a research career.

h)

> **Improving Participation and Interrater Agreement in Scoring Ambulatory Pediatric Association Abstracts**
>
> *How Well Have We Succeeded?*

Usually the part of the article that one reads first is the abstract or the summary. In American journals it usually comprises four parts:

Conclusions
Methods
Objective(s)
Results

Put the headings in the order you would expect them to appear.

Task 23

Here is the Summary of the article from Task 21. Complete the text by putting in the appropriate headings and missing words. Each gap can be completed by adding either one word, or one word plus an article (*the*, *a* or *an*).

..........................(1): To determine whether increasing the number and types of interrater agreement in scoring abstracts submitted ....(2) Ambulatory Pediatric Association.

..........................(3): In 1990, all abstracts were rated by each ....(4) 11 members of the board of directors ....(5) Ambulatory Pediatric Association. In 1995, abstracts were reviewed ....(6) four to five raters, including eight members of the board of directors, two chairpersons of special interest groups, and ten regional chairpersons, for a total of 20 potential reviewers. Submissions were divided into the following three categories ....(7) review: emergency medicine, behavioural pediatrics, and general pediatrics. Weighted percentage agreement and weighted K scores were computed for 1990 and 1995 abstract scores.

..........................(8): Between 1990 and 1995, the number of abstracts submitted ....(9) Ambulatory Pediatric Association increased from 246 to 407, the number ....(10) reviewers increased from 11 to 20, the weighted percentage agreement between raters remained approximately 79% and weighted K scores remained less ....(11) 0.25. Agreement was not significantly better for the emergency medicine and behavioural abstracts than for general pediatrics, ...(12) was it better for the raters ....(13) reviewed fewer abstracts than those who reviewed many.

..........................(14): The number and expertise ....(15) those rating abstracts increased from 1990 to 1995. ....(16), interrater agreement did ....(17) change and remained low. Further efforts are needed ....(18) improve the interrater agreement.

Think about some of the journal articles that you regularly read. Do they follow the same structure, or are there some differences? Compare notes with a partner or other members of your group.

If you have the opportunity, visit the medical library, or a library that has some medical and scientific journals and compare their structures. How do they compare with the structures of journal articles written in your mother tongue?

Task 24

Mr Hudson was put on a waiting list for a TURP following his consultation with Mr Fielding. However, after five weeks he was admitted to hospital as an emergency. Study the registrar's case notes on Mr Hudson following his admission.

PRESENT COMPLAINT
Unable to PU for 24hrs
In severe pain
Awaiting TURP for enlarged prostate

O/E
General Condition — Restlessness due to pain
Sweating ++

ENT

RS — Chest clear

CVS — P120 — AF
BP $\frac{180}{120}$ — HS I, II no murmurs

GIS — bladder distended to umbilicus

GUS — PR prostate enlarged, soft

CNS — NAD

DIAGNOSIS
(1) Acute retention due to prostate hypertrophy
(2) Atrial fibrillation ? cause

MANAGEMENT
Sedate
Catheterise
Ask physician to see him

The following notes were added after catheterisation:

INVESTIGATIONS
urinalysis 3+ sugar

MANAGEMENT
R_x digoxin 0.25 mg daily
metformin 500 mg t.d.s.

What addition would you make to the Diagnosis section?
Write a letter to Mr Hudson's doctor, Dr Watson, explaining your findings.

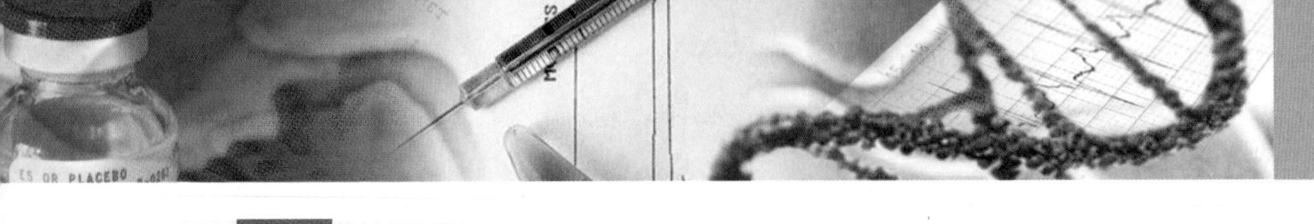

5 Investigations

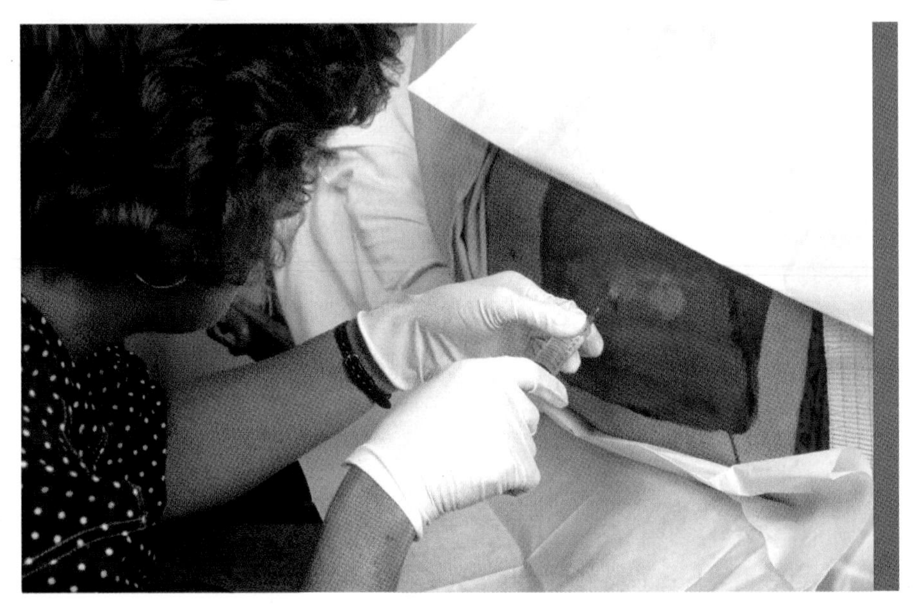

Section 1 Explaining and discussing investigations

Task 1

In Task 2 you will hear a hospital doctor preparing a patient for a lumbar puncture. The patient has been ill for a week with headaches and a temperature following a respiratory infection. Examination shows neck stiffness. During the extract the doctor instructs the patient to take up the correct position for the lumbar puncture. Try to predict her instructions from these clues. Each blank may represent one or several missing words.

1 Now I want you to move right to the edge of the bed.

2 Lie on ....

3 Now can you bend both your ....?

4 Put your head ....

5 Curl ....

6 Lie ....

Task 2

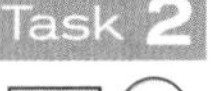

Listen to the extract and check your predictions.

Language focus 12

In the extract on the previous page the doctor tries to do three things.

1 Explain what she is going to do and why.
   - *Now I'm going to* take some fluid off your back to find out what's giving you these headaches.

2 Instruct the patient to take up the correct position.
   - *Now I want you to* move right to the edge of the bed.

3 Reassure the patient about the investigation.
   - *It won't take very long.*
   - Now I'm going to give you a local anaesthetic *so it won't be sore.*

Task 3

Here is part of a doctor's explanation during a sternal marrow investigation. The explanation has been put in the wrong order. Try to rearrange it.

a) Now I'm going to give you an injection of local anaesthetic. First into the skin and then into the bone.

b) Then we'll put a dressing over the area.

c) Now the next thing I'm going to do is to put a towel, a clean towel, over the area.

d) First of all, I'm just going to wash the area with a bit of antiseptic.

e) Just going to remove the needle from your chest.

f) Now we're ready to do the actual test.

g) Now I'm going to remove the actual cells from your bone.

Language focus 13

Doctors often combine reassurance with a warning. Study these examples from a sternal marrow investigation:

- It shouldn't be painful, *but you will be aware of a feeling of pressure.*
- *This may feel a little bit uncomfortable,* but it won't take long.

Task 4

Work in pairs. Practise preparing a patient for the following investigations. Explain, instruct, reassure and warn where necessary.

1 ECG / man, 68 / ? myocardial infarction

2 barium meal / woman, 23 / ? duodenal ulcer

3 Crosby capsule / girl, 6 / ? coeliac disease

4 ultrasound scan / woman, 26 / baby small for dates at 32 weeks

5 myelogram / man, 53 / carpenter / ? prolapsed intervertebral disc

When you have finished, compare your explanations and instructions with the recording.

Task 5

Study this list of investigations for a 43-year-old salesman who presents with a blood pressure of 200 over 130. Then list them in the three categories below.

barium meal
chest X-ray
creatinine
ECG
IVP (IVU)
MRI scan of the brain
radioisotope studies
serum cholesterol
serum thyroxine
urea and electrolytes
uric acid
urinalysis

Essential	*Possibly useful*	*Not required*

Now listen to three doctors discussing this case and the investigations. Note how they group the investigations. Have you grouped them in the same way?

Language focus 14

Note these expressions used *between doctors* in discussing a choice of investigations.

Essential	*Possibly useful*	*Not required*
should must be + required essential important indicated	could	need not be + not necessary not required not important
Essential not to do		
should not must not be + contraindicated		

For example:

- The patient *should* be given an X-ray.
- *It is important* to give an X-ray.
- An X-ray *is indicated* (formal).

Task 6

Study these brief case notes and choose only the most appropriate investigations from the list which follows each case. Add any other investigations you think essential.

Then work in pairs. Take three cases each. Explain to each other your choice of investigations for these patients.

1

SURNAME Cumley		FIRST NAMES John
AGE 60	SEX M	MARITAL STATUS M
OCCUPATION Electrician		
PRESENT COMPLAINT Coughing up blood. Has temp. Smoker.		
O/E General Condition finger clubbing, air entry L mid zone		

chest X-ray
sputum culture
bronchoscopy
serum proteins
urinalysis

2

SURNAME Sharp		FIRST NAMES Emma
AGE 43	SEX F	MARITAL STATUS M
OCCUPATION Housewife		
PRESENT COMPLAINT abdominal pain, heavy periods		
O/E General Condition		

pelvic ultrasound
chest X-ray
Hb
LFTS
EUA and D & C

3

SURNAME Donaldson		FIRST NAMES Grace
AGE 23	SEX F	MARITAL STATUS S
OCCUPATION Schoolteacher		
PRESENT COMPLAINT agitation, difficulty in sleeping, ↑ appetite ↓ wt		
O/E General Condition warm, sweaty skin, tachycardia, soft goitre with bruit		

angiogram
CAT scan of skull
serum thyroxine
TSH

4

SURNAME Pritt		FIRST NAMES William
AGE 44	SEX M	MARITAL STATUS D
OCCUPATION Printer		
PRESENT COMPLAINT abdominal pain after eating fatty foods		
O/E General Condition obese ++, tender R hypochondrium		

cholecystogram
MSU
barium meal
ECG
endoscopy
abdominal ultrasound

5

SURNAME *Scott*		FIRST NAMES *Barry*	
AGE *2 1/2*	SEX *M*	MARITAL STATUS	
OCCUPATION *–*			
PRESENT COMPLAINT *sore throat, mother says he has a temp. and rash*			
O/E General Condition *occipital glands enlarged and tender, maculopapular rash behind ears and spreading down trunk*			

chest X-ray
throat swab
serum iron
monospot
viral antibodies
full blood count

6

SURNAME *Lock*		FIRST NAMES *Mary*	
AGE *68*	SEX *F*	MARITAL STATUS *Sep*	
OCCUPATION *Retired waitress*			
PRESENT COMPLAINT *dull ache above R eye, sees haloes round lights*			
O/E General Condition *hazy cornea, pupil half-dilated and fixed*			

tonometry
skull X-ray
swab from cornea to bacteriology

Work in pairs. Student B should start.

A: Play the part of the patient for one of the six cases above. In case 5 you are a parent. You want to know why the investigations are required, what the investigations involve, and if the investigations will be painful.

B: Play the part of the doctor. Explain the investigations required and answer any questions raised.

When you have finished, compare your explanations with the recording.

Section 2 Using medical documents

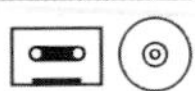

Listen to this telephone call from a haematology lab to a doctor's surgery. As you listen, record the results of the investigations in the correct spaces on the form below. The patient is Mr Kevin Hall (see Unit 1, pp. 5 and 9).

TELEPHONE REPORT FROM HAEMATOLOGY LABORATORY

PATIENT'S NAME **UNIT NO**

....

	BLOOD FILM
WBC $\times 10^9$/L	NEUTRO .... %
Hb g/dl	LYMPH .... %
Hct	MONO .... %
MCVfl	EOSINO .... %
Platelets $\times 10^9$/L	BASO .... %
ESR mm	

OTHER INFORMATION

....

....

....

PROTHROMBIN RATIO .... :1

TIME MESSAGE RECEIVED .... AM/PM

MESSAGE RECEIVED BY ....

DATE RECEIVED ....

Task 9

Study the clinical chemistry results for Mr Hall which are shown on the form below. In addition to these results, the patient's urine showed: albumen ++, and a trace of glucose.

DEPARTMENT OF CLINICAL BIOCHEMISTRY
SOUTHERN GENERAL HOSPITAL, NHS TRUST

GP 5487 HALL, KEVIN 30/04/67 M
DR WATSON HEALTH CENTRE, NEWTOWN

Date Collected	25/05/99
Time "	00.00
Date Received	25/05/99
Time "	13.15
Spec No.	74627

S/Pl SODIUM (135–145) mmol/l	158
S/Pl POTASSIUM (3.6–5) mmol/l	6.2
S/Pl CHLORIDE (95–105) mmol/l	96
S/Pl CO2 (21–26) mmol/l	16
Serum/Pl UREA (3.3–6.6) mmol/l	50.1
TOTAL PROTEIN (60–80) s/l	71
S/Pl CREATININE (60–120) μmol/l	90
S/Pl GLUCOSE (3.6–5.8)	5.1

COMMENTS

Report printed on 26-May-99 8:38:30

Identify which of these results are outside the normal range and describe each of the significant results. These words may be useful:

low high abnormal
reduced raised
elevated

For example:

– *Blood urea is abnormally high.*

Task 10 

Kevin Hall's GP phones the hospital to arrange for his admission. Fill in the gaps in his call using the information from the haematology lab, the clinical chemistry results, and the information given in Task 9. Add your own diagnosis.

DOCTOR: I'm phoning about a 32-year-old man. I saw him a year ago when he ....(1) of headaches which had been troubling him for three months. On examination he was ....(2) to have a blood pressure of 180 over 120. Urinalysis was ....(3), ECG and chest X-rays were also normal. He was commenced on a beta ....(4) and ....(5) but his blood pressure remained slightly ....(6).

On a recent visit he complained of nausea, vomiting and headaches. His blood pressure was 160 over 120, urinalysis showed ....(7) plus plus and a trace of glucose. I've just received his lab results. His haemoglobin is ....(8), ESR ....(9). Blood film showed poikilocytosis plus and ....(10) cells plus plus. Blood urea was ....(11) raised, ...(12), sodium 158, potassium 6.2, bicarbonate ....(13).

I'd like to arrange his urgent admission for investigation and treatment of ....(14).

Look back at the case of Peter Green in Unit 1, p. 10. Reread the letter from his GP and his case notes. List the investigations you would carry out on this patient. Then study the following haematological, clinical chemistry and ECG (V5 only) results for Mr Green. Write to his GP, Dr Chapman, and describe your findings.

Department of Clinical and Laboratory Haematology
Southern General Hospital

A1563526 GREEN, PETER 08/08/58 M
DR CHAPMAN HEALTH CENTRE, APPLECROSS

Date	07/10/00						
Time	10.59						
Specimen No.	0462Q						
Haemoglobin (120–180 g/l)	148						
Haematocrit (40%–54%)	43.1						
Mean Cell Vol (78–98 fl)	100						
Platelet Count ($150–400 \times 10^9$/l)	264						
Total WBC ($4–11 \times 10^9$/l)	7.1						
Differential WBC							
Neutrophils ($2.0–7.5 \times 10^9$/l)	7.4						
Lymphocytes ($1.5–4.0 \times 10^9$/l)	1.7						
Monocytes ($0.2–0.8 \times 10^9$/l)	0.6						
Eosinophils ($<0.7–10^9$/l)	0.1						
Basophils ($<0.2 \times 10^9$/l)	0.0						
Myelocytes							
Promyelocytes							
Blast Cells							
NRBC/100 WBC							
E.S.R. (1mm–9mm/hr)							
Reticulocytes ($10–100 \times 10^9$/l)							
Blood film comment/Results:							

(REMOVE APPROPRIATE PREVIOUS REPORT BEFORE FILING IN CASE NOTES)

DEPARTMENT OF CLINICAL BIOCHEMISTRY
SOUTHERN GENERAL HOSPITAL, NHS TRUST

GP 1563526 GREEN, PETER 08/08/58 M
DR CHAPMAN HEALTH CENTRE, NEWTOWN

Date Collected	07/10/00
Time "	00.00
Date Received	07/10/00
Time "	16.13
Spec No.	35931

S/Pl SODIUM (135–145) mmol/l	137
S/Pl POTASSIUM (3.6–5) mmol/l	4.6
S/Pl CHLORIDE (95–105) mmol/l	96
S/Pl CO2 (21–26) mmol/l	22
Serum/Pl UREA (3.3–6.6) mmol/l	3.6
TOTAL PROTEIN (60–80) s/l	71
S/Pl CHOLEST'OL (3.9–6.2) mmol/l	7.2
S/Pl TRIGLYC'DE (.8–2.1) mmol/l	1.61
HDL CHOLESTEROL (.9–1.4) mmol/l	1.09

COMMENTS

Report printed on 07-Oct-00 12:27:30

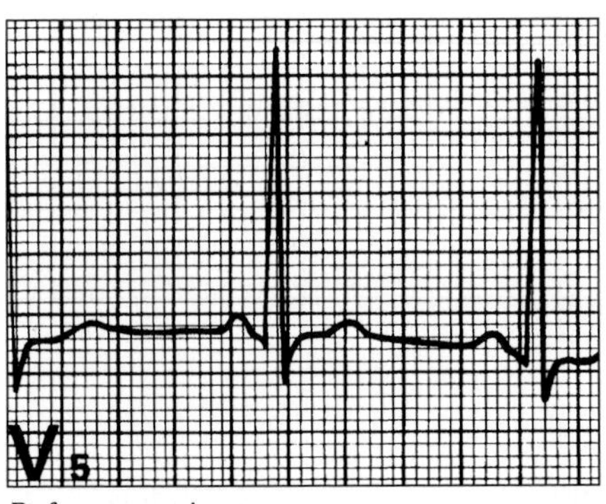

Before exercise

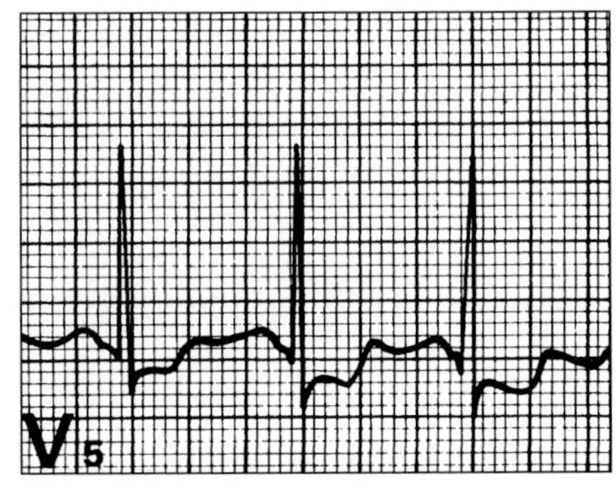

Immediately after exercise

Task 12 These headings are commonly used in British medical journals. Number them in the order you would expect them to feature.

Results
Summary
Discussion
Patients and methods
References
Introduction
Authors
Title

Task 13 These brief extracts from an article in *The Lancet* are listed in the order in which many medical researchers read such articles. Use the list given in Task 12 to identify which parts of the article they are taken from so that you can work out this reading procedure.

a)

Medical Research Council randomised trial of endometrial resection versus hysterectomy in management of menorrhagia

b)

Background The most frequent indication for hysterectomy is menorrhagia, even though the uterus is normal in a large number of patients. Transcervical resection of the endometrium (TCRE) is a less drastic alternative, but success rates have varied and menorrhagia can recur. We have tested the hypothesis that the difference in the proportion of women dissatisfied and requiring further surgery within 3 years of TCRE or hysterectomy would be no more than 15%.

Methods 202 women with symptomatic menorrhagia were recruited to a multicentre, randomised, controlled trial to compare the two interventions. TCRE and hysterectomy were randomly assigned in a ratio of two to one. The primary endpoints were women's satisfaction and need for further surgery. The patients' psychological and social states were monitored before surgery, then annually with a questionnaire. Analysis was by intention to treat.

Findings Data were available for 172 women (56 hysterectomy, 116 TCRE); 26 withdrew before surgery and four were lost to follow-up. Satisfaction scores were higher for hysterectomy than for TCRE throughout follow-up (median 2 years), but the differences were not significant (at 3 years 27 [96%] of 28 in hysterectomy group *vs* 46 [85%] of 54 in TCRE group were satisfied; p=0·16). 25 (22%) women in the TCRE group and five (9%) in the hysterectomy group required further surgery (relative risk 0·46 [95% CI 0·2–1·1], p=0·053). TCRE had the benefits of shorter operating time, fewer complications, and faster rates of recovery.

Interpretation TCRE is an acceptable alternative to hysterectomy in the treatment of menorrhagia for many women with no other serious disorders.

c)

Greenbury[25] showed a high rate of psychiatric morbidity in patients attending gynaecological outpatient clinics with a complaint of menorrhagia, whereas Gath and colleagues[26] showed the beneficial influence of hysterectomy on patients with this disorder. Our study has confirmed these observations and has also shown that TCRE has an equally positive effect on psychosocial wellbeing in women with menorrhagia.

So how does TCRE compare with hysterectomy? Whereas the use of TCRE as an alternative to hysterectomy has been questioned,[27,28] our results show that for most women who have menorrhagia with no other serious pathology, TCRE is a genuine alternative to hysterectomy.

e)

Endometrial ablation with electrosurgery, laser, or other forms of thermal energy has been introduced as a less invasive alternative to hysterectomy in the management of abnormal uterine bleeding of benign aetiology.[1] Medical treatment of menorrhagia is often ineffective. Hysterectomy is the most common major surgical

f)

Hugh O'Connor, J A Mark Broadbent, Adam L Magos, K McPherson

d)

	Hysterectomy (n=56)	TCRE (n=116)	p value
Number of cases with follow-up data			
Year 1	46/52 (88%)	104/112 (93%)	
Year 2	38/45 (84%)	86/98 (88%)	
Year 3	28/30 (93%)	54/61 (89%)	
Satisfied with outcome of surgery			
Year 1	42/46 (91%)	90/104 (87%)	0·59
Year 2	36/38 (94%)	74/86 (86%)	0·22
Year 3	27/28 (96%)	46/54 (85%)	0·16

Table 4: **Follow-up details**

g)

1 Magos AL. Management of menorrhagia. *BMJ* 1990; **300:** 1537–38.
2 Vessey MP, Villard-Mackintosh L, McPherson K, Coulter A, Yeates D. The epidemiology of hysterectomy: findings in a large cohort study. *Br J Obstet Gynaecol* 1992; **99:** 402–07.
3 Magos AL, Baumann R, Turnbull AC. Transcervical resection of endometrium in women with menorrhagia. *BMJ* 1989; **298:** 1209–12.
4 Maher PJ, Hill DJ. Transcervical endometrial resection for abnormal uterine bleeding: report of 100 cases and review of the literature. *Aust N Z J Obstet Gynaecol* 1990; **30:** 357–60.
5 Derman SG, Rehnstrom J, Neuwirth RS. Long-term effectiveness of

Task 14

This is an extract from the part that a researcher chose to read next. Which part is it? Complete the extract by adding one word for each gap.

Patients were randomly assigned hysterectomy ....(1) TCRE at the time ....(2) recruitment in the clinic, ...(3) most cases several weeks ....(4) their planned surgery. Individuals ....(5) assigned TCRE and hysterectomy in a ratio of two ....(6) one because little information ....(7) available about the hysteroscopic procedure and ....(8) protocol was felt to assist recruitment. ....(9) computer-generated random-number sequence was used, ...(10) code for which was kept ....(11) the Royal Free Hospital, London. When ....(12) appointments for surgery, the recruiting physician telephoned ....(13) coordinating centre and ....(14) were given the next treatment ....(15) the randomisation schedule. Patients were fully counselled ....(16) TCRE and hysterectomy before ....(17) were asked to give their consent ....(18) randomisation. The study was approved ....(19) the ethics committees at ....(20) the participating hospitals.

Task 15

Mr Hudson had a transurethral resection of his prostate. His diabetes was controlled by diet and oral hypoglycaemic drugs. He continued with digoxin. The diuretic was discontinued. Four months later he complained of diarrhoea and sickness over a period of two days. He was treated for this, but four days later a neighbour called Mr Hudson's doctor as an emergency. The doctor arranged an immediate admission and wrote a letter to the hospital consultant to accompany Mr Hudson to hospital. Complete the gaps in the letter on p.64 with the help of the GP's case notes given below.

PRESENT COMPLAINT
Diarrhoea and vomiting for 6 days.

O/E
General Condition dehydrated and semi-comatose

ENT NAD

RS NAD

CVS P irreg. 110/min BP 110/60

GIS Sl. distension of abdo. No tenderness.
Bowel sounds absent.

GUS NAD

CNS Difficulty to arouse. Responds to painful stimuli.

IMMEDIATE PAST HISTORY
Diabetic on metformin 500 mg t.d.s
and digoxin 0.25 mg for CCF. TURP 4/12 ago.

POINTS OF NOTE

INVESTIGATIONS

DIAGNOSIS
? diabetic coma following acute gastroenteritis

Dear Mr Fielding,

Thank you for arranging to admit Mr Hudson. He is a 66-year-old widower who has had ....(1) and vomiting for six days. He is a diabetic on ....(2), 500 mg, ...(3) times daily and also takes digoxin for mild ....(4) failure. When our nurse visited him four days ago, his general condition was good but when I called to see him today, I found him ....(5) and ....(6). He still has diarrhoea although vomiting has stopped. He is apyrexial, blood pressure is 110/60 and his pulse weak and ....(7) at 110 per minute. The ....(8) is slightly distended although there is no ....(9). Bowel sounds are ....(10).

Diagnosis: ? acute gastroenteritis leading to ....(11) diabetic coma. By the way, he had a ....(12) four months ago which was uncomplicated.

Yours sincerely,

Dr Peter Watson

Work in pairs. Student B should start.

A: Play the part of the consultant. Explain briefly the investigations you intend to carry out on Mr Hudson and his present condition.

B: Play the part of Mr Hudson's son or daughter. You are concerned about your father. Find out what is wrong with him and ask what the consultant is going to do to help your father.

When you have finished, compare your explanations with the recording.

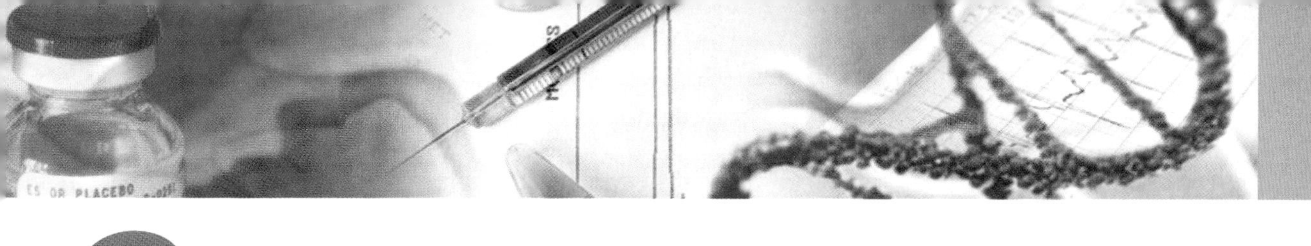

6 Making a diagnosis

Section 1 Discussing a diagnosis

Task 1

You will hear an extract in which a doctor interviews a 59-year-old office worker. As you listen, note the patient's present complaint.

SURNAME Nicol		FIRST NAMES Harvey
AGE 59	SEX M	MARITAL STATUS M
OCCUPATION Office worker		
PRESENT COMPLAINT		

Complete Tasks 2, 3 and 4 before you check your answers in the Key.

Task 2

Listen to the extract again and write down several possible diagnoses for this patient. You will be given further information on him later.

....

....

....

Complete Tasks 3 and 4 before you check your answers in the Key.

Here are the doctor's findings on examination.

O/E

General Condition

Good — T 37.4°

ENT

RS

CVS — P 80/min reg. — BP 160/95
HS normal — left temporal artery palpable

GIS

GUS

CNS — No neck stiffness. Fundi normal.
Neck movts full with no pain.

Look back at the possible diagnoses you listed in Task 2. Order them so that the most likely diagnosis is first and the least likely last. Exclude any which now seem very unlikely.

....
....
....

Which investigations would you check for this patient? Write them here.

INVESTIGATIONS

Complete Task 4 before you check your answers in the Key.

The results of some investigations for this patient are given on p. 75. How do these findings affect your diagnosis? Write your final diagnosis here.

DIAGNOSIS

Language focus 15

Note these expressions used *between doctors* in discussing a diagnosis.

	Certain	*Fairly certain*	*Uncertain*
Yes	is must	seems probably likely	might could may
No	can't definitely not exclude rule out	unlikely	possibly a possibility

The listening extract in Tasks 1 and 2 provides little information on which to base our diagnosis. We are still uncertain. We can say:

- The patient *might* have cervical spondylosis.
- Cervical spondylosis is a *possibility*.

The findings on examination provide more evidence. Some diagnoses become more likely while others become less likely. We can say:

- He *seems* to have temporal arteritis.
- There is no neck stiffness. It's *unlikely* that he's got cervical spondylosis.

The results of the investigations provide stronger evidence for our final diagnosis. We can say:

- A raised ESR makes temporal arteritis *very likely*.
- Normal MRI scan *excludes* a space-occupying lesion.
- He *can't* have a space-occupying lesion.

Finally, following the biopsy, we can say:

- He *must* have temporal arteritis.

Task 5

Work in pairs. Try to make a diagnosis on the basis of the information given on each patient. The exercise is in three stages. At each stage you are given more information to help you make a final diagnosis. Discuss your diagnoses at each stage.

STAGE A

1 The patient is a 26-year-old woman complaining of swelling of the ankles.

2 The patient is a 5-year-old girl with a petechial rash.

3 The patient is a 28-year-old man with headaches, sore throat and enlarged glands in the neck.

4 The patient is a 40-year-old woman complaining of nausea and episodes of pain in the right hypochondrium.

5 The patient is a 49-year-old man exhibiting Raynaud's phenomenon and with difficulty in swallowing.

Do not look ahead until you have considered a diagnosis for each patient.

STAGE B

1 Pregnancy test is negative. Chest X-ray is normal. Pulse is normal. The liver is not enlarged.
2 Both ankles, the left elbow and the right wrist are swollen and painful. The history shows no ingestion of drugs. Bone marrow is normal.
3 The spleen is palpable and there is a maculopapular rash all over.
4 The pain is associated with dietary indiscretion. Murphy's sign is positive. There is mild jaundice.
5 The patient exhibits cutaneous calcinosis and has difficulty in breathing.

Do not look ahead until you have considered a diagnosis for each patient.

STAGE C

1 Five day fecal fat collection is 15 mmol/l. Jejunal biopsy is normal. Lab stick urinary protein test shows protein ++. Serum total protein is 40 g/l.
2 The rash is on the buttocks and extensor surfaces of the arms and legs.
3 WBC shows lymphocytes ++. Monospot is positive.
4 Lab tests show alkaline phosphatase 160 units/l. USS shows a non-functioning gall bladder.
5 The patient's face is pinched.

Section 2 Explaining a diagnosis

Look back at Task 1 in Unit 3, p. 28. In that extract a doctor was examining a patient, Mr Jameson, suffering from leg and back pain. An MRI scan of the lumbar spine confirmed that the patient had a prolapsed intervertebral disc. Think about how you would explain this diagnosis to the patient. Write down the points you would include in your explanation. List the points in the best order. For example:

1 how serious the problem is

You will hear the doctor explaining the diagnosis to the patient. As you listen, note the points covered and the order in which they are dealt with. Then compare this with your own list in Task 6.

Language focus 16

When explaining a diagnosis, a patient would expect you to answer the following questions:

1 What's the cause of my problem?
2 How serious is it?
3 What are you going to do about it?
4 What are the chances of a full recovery?

In Unit 7, we will deal with questions 3 and 4. Here we will look at some of the language used to answer questions 1 and 2.

In explanations it is important to use straightforward, non-specialist language with only such detail as is important for the patient's understanding of the problem. The language of the textbooks you may have studied is clearly unsuitable for patient explanation. Compare this extract with the recorded explanation in Task 7.

> Herniation of part of a lumbar intervertebral disc is a common cause of combined back pain and sciatica ... Part of the gelatinous nucleus pulposus protrudes through a rent in the annulus fibrosus at its weakest part, which is postero-lateral ... If it is large, the protrusion herniates through the posterior ligament and may impinge upon an issuing nerve to cause sciatic pain.
>
> (J. C. Adams, *Outline of Orthopaedics*, 10th ed. (Edinburgh: Churchill Livingstone, 1986), p. 217.)

You can make sure your explanations are easily understood by avoiding medical terminology where possible and defining the terms you use in a simple way.
Note how the doctor describes a disc:

– *The disc is a little pad of gristle which lies between the bones in your spine.*

Task 8

Write simple explanations for patients of these terms. Compare your explanations with those of other students.

1 the pancreas
2 the thyroid
3 fibroids
4 emphysema
5 arrhythmia
6 bone marrow
7 the prostate gland
8 gastro-oesophageal reflux

Language focus 17

Explanations often involve describing causes and effects. Look at these examples:

Cause	*Effect*
bend the knee	the tension is taken off the nerve
straighten it	the nerve goes taut

We can link a cause and an effect like this:

– *If we bend the knee, the tension is taken off the nerve.*
– *If we straighten it, the nerve goes taut.*

Note that both the cause and effect are in the present tense because we are describing something which is generally true.

Task 9

Write a suitable effect for each of these causes. Then link each cause and effect to make a simple statement you could use in an explanation to a patient.

1 The stomach produces too much acid.
2 A woman gets German measles during pregnancy.
3 You vomit several times in quick succession.
4 Your skin is in contact with certain plants.
5 Your blood pressure remains high.
6 You give your baby too much fruit.
7 The cholesterol level in the blood gets too high.
8 There are repeated injuries to a joint.

Task 10

How would you explain these diagnoses to the following patients or their relatives? Work in pairs. Student A should start.

A: Play the part of the doctor. Explain these diagnoses to the patients or their relatives below.

B: Play the part of the patients. In 2 and 6, play the part of a parent, and in 5 play the part of the son or daughter.

1 A 33-year-old salesman suffering from a duodenal ulcer.
2 A 6-year-old boy with Perthes' disease, accompanied by his parents.
3 A 21-year-old professional footballer with a torn meniscus of the right knee.
4 A 43-year-old teacher with fibroids.
5 An 82-year-old retired nurse suffering from dementia, accompanied by her son and daughter.

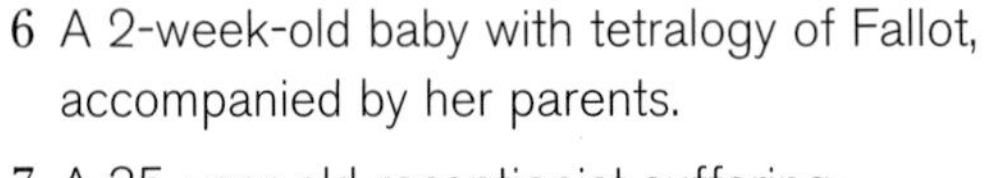

6 A 2-week-old baby with tetralogy of Fallot, accompanied by her parents.
7 A 35-year-old receptionist suffering from hypothyroidism.

When you have finished, compare your explanations with the recording.

Task 11

Here are some extracts from an article in the *British Journal of General Practice* given in the order in which they were read. Try to identify them to work out the procedure used and suggest a suitable title. The complete article has these components:

Title
Authors
Authors' affiliations
Summary
Introduction
Method
Results
Discussion
References

a)

Background. *The proportion of female general practitioners is steadily increasing.*
Aim. *To compare male and female general practitioners with respect to their job satisfaction and professional commitments within and outside their practices.*
Method. *A questionnaire was sent to all 896 general practitioner principals with patients in Staffordshire in 1994. The main elements were: job satisfaction (on a five-point scale) from eight possible sources; whether personal responsibility was taken for 12 different practice tasks; and professional commitments outside the practice.*
Results. *A total of 620 (69%) general practitioners responded. Female doctors derived more satisfaction than male doctors from relationships with patients (P = 0.002). Female doctors were more likely to be working in training practices, and were likely to be on-call less and to work fewer sessions. Male general practitioners were more likely to take lead responsibility for practice computers, minor surgery, meeting external visitors and finance, whereas female practitioners were more likely to be responsible for looking after women patients' health.*
Conclusion. *Considerable differences were found between male and female general practitioners. These differences are likely to have an increasing impact as the percentage of female general practitioners continues to rise.*

Keywords: general practitioners; job satisfaction; gender differences; work.

b)

Women doctors derived more job satisfaction than men from their relationships with patients. This ties in with research from Australia,[16] where a survey of 500 GPs found that women were more likely to be orientated to relationships with patients than men, as well as being better able to identify and treat patients' psychosocial problems. But the largest differences in the survey were in the responsibilities for practice tasks. Women were more likely than men to be responsible for women patients' health and antenatal work, whereas men were more likely to be responsible for practice computers, minor surgery and several administrative tasks. It is difficult to determine to what extent these gender differences have arisen from personal aptitudes and preferences, or from confinement in traditional roles. The former would seem to be more acceptable than the latter. Howie *et al*[17] have demonstrated that GPs who are forced to deviate from their preferred styles at work are more likely to underperform and feel stressed.

All doctors of both genders should be given opportunities to develop as individuals, so that diversity is encouraged and the strengths of all doctors of both genders are fully exploited.

c)

Table 1. Practice characteristics of male and female general practitioners.

Practice characteristics:	Percentage of general practitioners Male (n = 481)	Female (n = 139)
Number of partners:		
single-handed	13	9
2 – 3	26	32
≥ 4	60	58
no response	0	1
Level of seniority		
single-handed	13	9
most senior	28	16
2nd	24	22
3rd	15	14
≥ 4th	16	34
all equal	1	4
no response	2	1
On-call frequency (days per month):		
never	2	17
≤ 4	12	27
5 – 8	55	28
≥ 9	28	21
no response	3	7
Half-days free from practice work:		
none	18	10
1,2	74	51
3,4	2	25
≥ 5	1	7
not known	5	6

Table 2. Comparison of male and female general practitioners' mean scores for satisfaction levels at work.

Aspect of satisfaction	Mean satisfaction score (range of answers 0 – 4*) Male (n = 481)	Female (n = 139)
Relationship with patients	2.9	3.2†
Ability to treat illness	2.9	3.0
Relationship with practice staff	2.7	2.8
Relationship with other doctors	2.6	2.7
Financial security	2.6	2.6
Public view of profession	1.6	1.6
Own working conditions	2.3	2.3
Prevent illness by health promotion	1.3	1.4

*0 = not a source of satisfaction, ranging to 4 = extreme source of satisfaction.
†$P = 0.002$, Mann–Whitney test.
N.B. Non-response varied between 2 and 5% between questions.

Table 3. Percentage of male and female general practitioners who report that they themselves have lead responsibility for particular practice tasks in practices where there are partners of both genders (n = 363).

Task	Percentage of general practitioners claiming personal responsiblity Male (n = 250)	Female (n = 113)	P*
Computers	22	3	<0.0001
Minor surgery	24	8	0.0005
Practice finance	20	9	0.01
Practice administration	12	5	0.09
Women's health	1	31	<0.0001
Staff employment	10	4	0.07
Staff personal problems	12	16	0.5
Antenatal work	4	16	0.0005
Meeting external visitors	16	2	0.0002
Annual report	18	7	0.01
Health promotion	16	9	0.1
Buying equipment/stores	10	5	0.2

*P-value by χ^2 test.

d)

THE proportion of female medical students in the United Kingdom has risen steadily over the last 20 years so that medical school intakes now comprise similar numbers of men and women. Over half of all general practitioner (GP) registrars (trainees) are now female,[1] and the proportion of female GPs has increased from 19% in 1983 to 29% in 1993.

With the increasing numbers of female GPs, any gender differences between male and female GPs will become more important. These gender differences may include differences in career progression, job satisfaction, clinical and professional interests, mental health, assumptions of family responsibilities, extent of part-time working, and consulting styles.

Studies following up doctors who have completed their vocational training for general practice have found that nearly all doctors of both genders continue to work,[2] but that women are less likely to become principals than men[3] and are much more likely to be working as part-time principals.[2] These differences in the career progression of men and women doctors have been ascribed to gender-based stereotyping, to role strain and its impact on relationships, and to the lack of role models for women.[4,5]

Women GPs have been found to have greater overall job satisfaction than male GPs or to the general population.[6-9] Women GPs have been found to be more satisfied than their male colleagues with their hours of work,[7,8] recognition for good work,[7,8] freedom to choose methods of working[7,8] and psychosocial aspects of care,[9] whereas male GPs tend to be more satisfied with the organizational aspects of their work.[9] Lower rates of job satisfaction are important not only from the point of view of the individual doctor, but also because of the association with mental and physical ill-health and increased sick leave.[10]

Little work has been published about the influence of gender on the division of practice work between GP partners, but male GPs attending educational meetings have been found to elect for service management topics, whereas women are more likely to select health promotion meetings.[11] Considerably fewer female than male GPs seem to be involved in teaching or training.[3]

This paper presents differences between male and female GPs in their practices, in sources of satisfaction at work, in professional commitments outside their practices, and in responsibilities for practice tasks.

e)

R Chambers, DM, FRCGP, general practitioner, Stone, and senior lecturer in primary health care, University of Keele. I Campbell, MD, FRCS, FRCR, medical statistics consultant, Wirral.
Submitted: 11 July 1995; accepted: 28 November 1995.

f)

1. Department of Health. *Statistics for general medical practitioners in England and Wales: 1983–1993*. Department of Health Statistical Bulletin, May 1994.
2. Allen I. *Part-time working in general practice*. London: Policy Studies Institute, 1992.
3. Johnson N, Hasler J, Mant D, *et al.* General practice careers: changing experience of men and women vocational trainees between 1974 and 1989. *Br J Gen Pract* 1993; 43: 141-145.
4. Allen I. *Doctors and their careers*. London: Policy Studies Institute, 1988.
5. Notman MT, Nadelson C. Medicine: a career conflict for women. *Am J Psychol* 1973; 130: 1123-1127.
6. Cooper CL, Rout U, Faragher B. Mental health, job satisfaction, and job stress among general practitioners. *BMJ* 1989: 298: 366-370.
7. Sutherland VJ, Cooper CL. Identifying distress among general practitioners: predictors of psychological ill-health and job dissatisfaction. *Soc Sci Med* 1993; 37: 575-581.
8. Rout U, Rout JK. Job satisfaction, mental health and job stress among general practitioners before and after the new contract — a comparative study. *Fam Pract* 1994; **11**: 300-306.
9. Branthwaite A, Ross A. Satisfaction and job stress in general practice. *Fam Pract* 1988; 5: 83-93.
10. Rees DW, Cooper CL. Occupational stress in health service employees. *Health Serv Man Res* 1990; 3: 163-172.
11. Murray, TS. Demographic characteristics of general practitioners attending educational meetings. *Br J Gen Pract* 1993; 43: 467-469.
12. Moses LE, Emerson JD, Hosseini H. Analysing data from ordered categories. *N Engl J Med* 1984; **311**: 442-448.
13. Armitage P, Berry G. *Statistical methods in medical research*, 2nd edn. Oxford: Blackwell Science, 1987.
14. Cooke M, Ronalds C. Women doctors in urban general practice: the doctors. *BMJ* 1985; 290: 755-758.
15. Firth-Cozens J, West MA. *Women at work: psychological and organisational perspectives*. Buckingham: Open University Press, 1991.
16. Britt, H, Bhasale, A, Miles DA, *et al. The gender of the general practitioner. Secondary analysis of data from the Australian morbidity and treatment survey in general practice 1990–1991*. Sydney: Family Medicine Research Unit, University of Sydney, 1994.
17. Howie JG, Hopton J, Heaney D, Porter A. Attitudes to medical care, the organization of work, and stress among general practitioners. *Br J Gen Pract* 1992; 42: 181-185.

Address for correspondence

Dr R Chambers, Centre for Primary Health Care, School of Postgraduate Medicine, University of Keele, Stoke Health Centre, Honeywall, Stoke-on-Trent ST4 7JB.

How do the results of this study compare with the situation in your country regarding the ratio of male to female GPs? Have another look at the tables and consider how they might compare.

Task 12

Complete this extract from the Method section of the same article by adding one word for each gap.

In June 1994, all 896 GP principals with patients ....(1) Staffordshire ....(2) sent a questionnaire. This included questions ....(3) the number of partners, the training status ....(4) the practice, the level ....(5) seniority, the number ....(6) half-days free of practice or medical commitments and the frequency ....(7) on-call duty. Enquiry was made ....(8) work done outside the practice and ....(9) participation in any professional committee(s). Subjects ....(10) asked to indicate ....(11) (if anyone) had special responsibility in their practice ....(12) a total of 12 activities, all of which would be expected to be carried ....(13) in every practice. Finally, eight questions ....(14) GPs' sources of satisfaction at work were derived ....(15) group discussions and background literature. Two discussion groups, one ....(16) eight women GPs and the second ....(17) 10 doctors of both genders, were held, the topic set being GPs' stress and job satisfaction. Eight possible sources ....(18) satisfaction..........................(19) identified, and for each ....(20) these, subjects were invited to respond ....(21) a five-point Likert scale, ranging from 'no' satisfaction to 'extreme' satisfaction (scale 0–4).

Questionnaires ....(22) despatched to individual practitioners via ....(23) family health services authority (FHA) courier system and completed forms ....(24) returned in freepost envelopes. Detachable code numbers ....(25) appended to the questionnaires to allow chasing ....(26) non-respondents, who were reminded twice.

Staffordshire FHSA was the responsible authority ....(27) 502 of the GPs. The other 304 GPs included ....(28) the survey had some patients residing in Staffordshire, ...(29) most of their patients lived in neighbouring counties and their responsible FHSA was one ....(30) the nine others neighbouring Staffordshire.

A Minitab package ....(31) used to process the responses. Tables of unordered categorical data ....(32) analysed by the chi-squared test. The Mann Whitney test ....(33) used for ordered categorical data when two groups were being compared; the Kruskal-Wallis test was used ....(34) three or more groups ....(35) being compared; these tests included an allowance ....(36) ties. The *P*-values calculated for these last two tests were two-sided. Cochran's technique was used to investigate whether some ....(37) the gender differences that ....(38) found were caused by confounding factors causing ....(39) spurious association.

Section 4 Case history: William Hudson

Look back at p. 64 to remind yourself of Mr Hudson's condition. Then work in pairs. Student A should start.

A: Play the part of a surgeon. You have performed a laparotomy on Mr Hudson. You find occlusion of the superior mesenteric artery and gangrene of the small bowel. You resect most of the small bowel. Explain to Mr Hudson's son or daughter what you have done.

B: Play the part of Mr Hudson's son or daughter. Ask the surgeon about your father's operation. Ask him or her to explain the cause of your father's problem. Also ask him or her what his chances are for the future.

When you have finished, compare your explanations with the recording.

Task 4 (see p. 66)

Results of investigations:

ESR – 80 mm in first hour
Neutrophils – 85%
Biopsy showed the changes of giant cell arteritis.

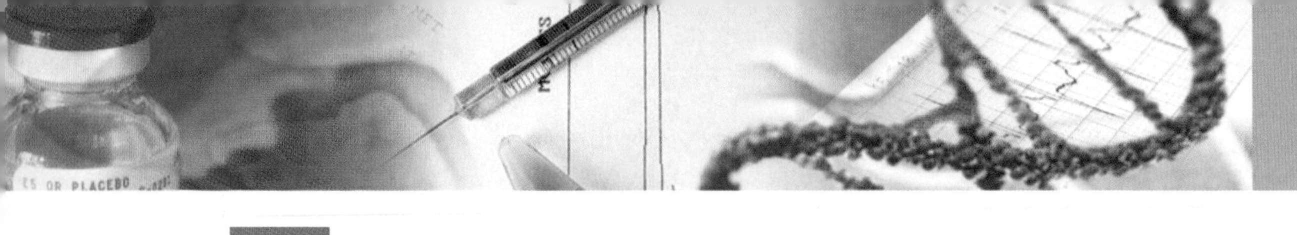

7 Treatment

Section 1 Medical treatment

Task 1

Look back at the case of Mr Jameson (see pp. 22–3, 28, 30–1, 44–5 and 68) and complete as much as you can of the case notes.

SURNAME *Jameson*	FIRST NAMES *Alan*
AGE *53* SEX *M*	MARITAL STATUS *M*
OCCUPATION *Carpenter*	
PRESENT COMPLAINT *Acute backache referred down R sciatic nerve distribution.*	
O/E General Condition *Fit, well-muscled.* ENT RS CVS GIS GUS CNS	
IMMEDIATE PAST HISTORY	

POINTS OF NOTE
Carpenter – active work.
1.78m, 68kg – tall, slightly-built.

INVESTIGATIONS

MRI – postero-lateral herniation of disc.

DIAGNOSIS

What treatment would you suggest?

Task 2

You will hear an extract from the consultation. Listen and complete the management section of the case notes.

MANAGEMENT
dihydrocodeine 2 q.d.s. p.c.

Language focus 18

Note how the doctor advises the patient about the following points:

The duration of the treatment:

– *You'll need* a few days off work …

How the patient must conduct himself during the treatment:

– *You should* rest for a day or two …

– *It's really not good to* rest for longer than that.

– *If you rest for a long time,* your muscles will get weaker and the pain will feel worse.

– *Don't* wait until the pain is out of control.

How would you advise each of these patients? Work in pairs. Student A should start.

A: Play the part of the doctor. Advise each of these patients about the treatment you plan for them.

B: Play the part of the patients. In 7, play the part of a parent.

1 A hypertensive 50-year-old director of a small company.

2 An insulin-dependent 11-year-old girl accompanied by her parents.

3 A 65-year-old schoolteacher with osteoarthritis of the left hip.

4 A 23-year-old sales representative affected by epilepsy.

5 A 52-year-old cook with carcinoma of the bowel.

6 A 27-year-old teacher of handicapped children suffering from a depressive illness.

7 A 6-month-old baby boy suffering from atopic eczema, accompanied by his parents.

When you have finished, compare your advice with the recording.

Here is the prescription that was given to Mr Jameson:

MR / MRS / MISS / Child } MR JAMESON
Surname of patient – in BLOCK LETTERS
ALAN
Initials and one full forename wherever possible
Age if under 12 years
YRS MTHS
Address 41 Mead Avenue
Edinburgh EH3 5EN
Pharmacist's Stamp
NP
NO. OF DAYS TREATMENT
N.B. ENSURE THAT DOSE IS STATED
For use only by Pricing Bureau

R_x
Tab. dihydrocodeine BP 30mg
Mitte 100 (one hundred tabs)
sig. 2 tablets, 6 hrly for pain, p.c.

Signature of Doctor
Date
For use by Pharmacist
IMPORTANT Read notes overleaf BEFORE going to the pharmacy. Medicine urgently required may be obtained outside normal hours if prescription is marked **Urgent** by the Doctor.

Which part of the prescription gives the following information?

a) how often the tablets should be taken

b) the purpose of the treatment

c) the amount prescribed

d) the name of the medicine

What do the following abbreviations stand for?

e) Mitte
f) tabs
g) sig.
h) p.c.

Task 5

Using the information given in Task 4, try to complete the doctor's instructions to Mr Jameson by putting one word in each gap.

DOCTOR: Now, Mr Jameson, here is a prescription for some ....(1) which you are to take..........(2) of every ....(3) hours. Try to take them ....(4) ....(5) if possible in case they cause you indigestion. You ....(6) take them during the night as well if you are awake with the ....(7).

When you have finished, listen to the recording.

Task 6

Try to match these treatments with the seven patients described in Task 3.

1 Tab. Naproxen 250 mg
Mitte 84
sig. 1 tab. t.i.d. c.c.

2 Tab. Paroxetine 20 mg
Mitte 30
sig. 1 tab. mane

3 Colostomy bags
Mitte 50

4 Human soluble insulin
100 IU/ml
Mitte 10 ml × 4
sig. 6 IU a.m.
sig. 4 IU p.m.

Human isophane insulin
100 IU/ml
Mitte 10 ml × 4
sig. 18 IU a.m.
sig. 8 IU p.m.

5 Tab. Atenolol 50 mg
Mitte 56
sig. 1 mane

6 Hydrocortisone cream 1%
Mitte 30 g
sig. apply thinly to the affected area b.i.d.

7 Tab. carbamazepine 400 mg
Mitte 60
sig. 1 tab. b.d.

What do the following abbreviations stand for?

a) b.i.d./b.d.
b) t.i.d./t.d.s.
c) c.c.
d) mane

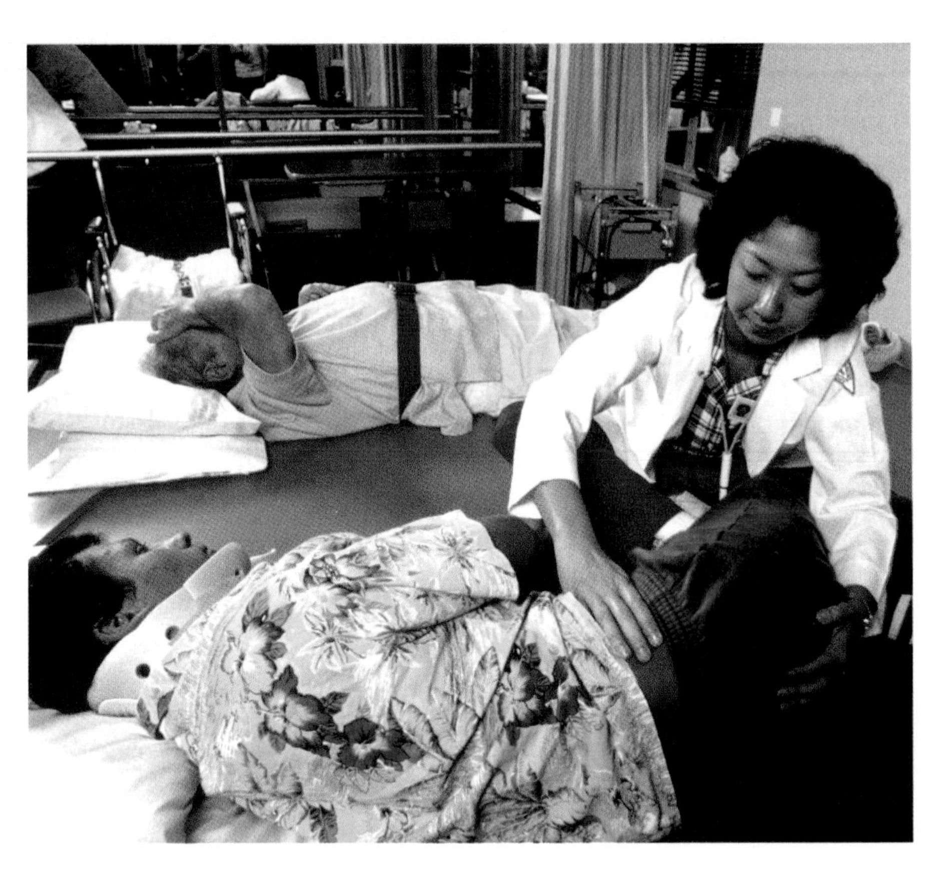

Task 7 

Listen carefully to the instructions that the physiotherapist gave Mr Jameson for his spinal extension exercises. Try to put these diagrams in the correct order using the instructions. Number them 1 to 5.

a)

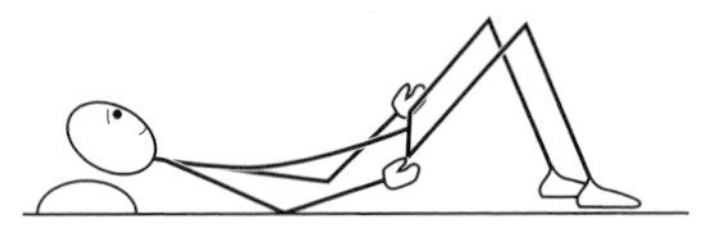

b)

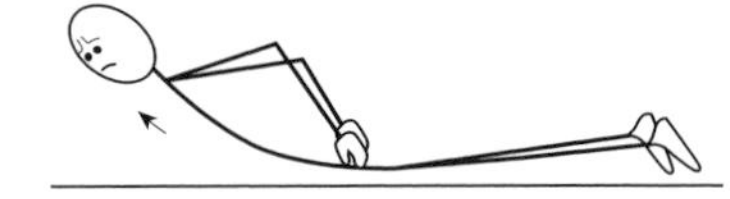

c)

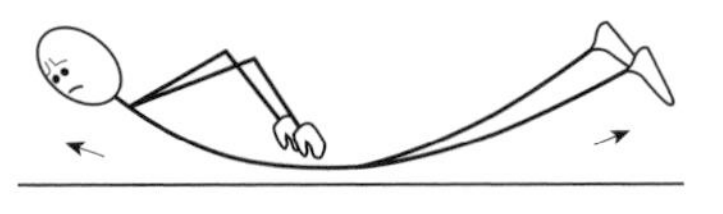

d)

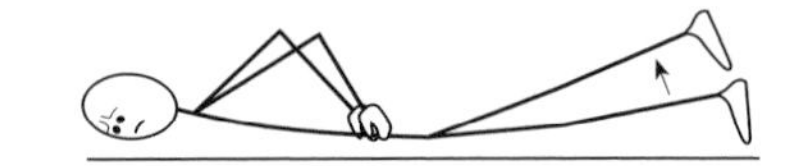

e)

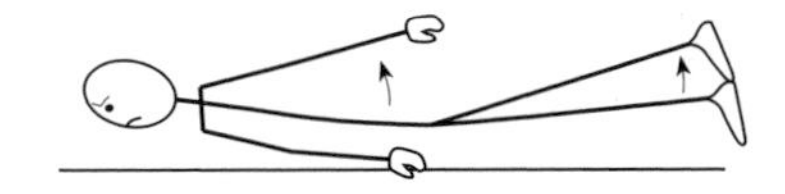

Language focus 19

Note how the physiotherapist marks the sequence of instructions:

- *First of all,* you lie down ...
- *Now* place your hands on your back ...

Read through the Tapescript for Task 8 (p. 103) and underline the markers of sequence used.

Note how the physiotherapist advises the patient:

- You *should* do these exercises three times a day, *preferably* on an empty stomach.
- You *should try to do* them as slowly and smoothly as possible ...

Note how the physiotherapist cautions the patient:

- You should *try to avoid jerking* your body.

Task 8

Complete these instructions to Mr Jameson using appropriate language.

1 .... on a hard surface.

2 .... careful while getting out of bed. .... roll over and then get up from your side.

3 .... bending forward, for example, if you are picking up something off the floor.

4 .... to bend your knees and keep your back straight.

5 .... lifting heavy weights.

Task 9

Work in pairs. Using the diagrams in Task 7 as cues, take turns at instructing Mr Jameson on each of these spinal exercises. Remember to use sequence markers and the correct verb forms.

When you have finished, compare your instructions with the recording.

Section 3 Surgical treatment

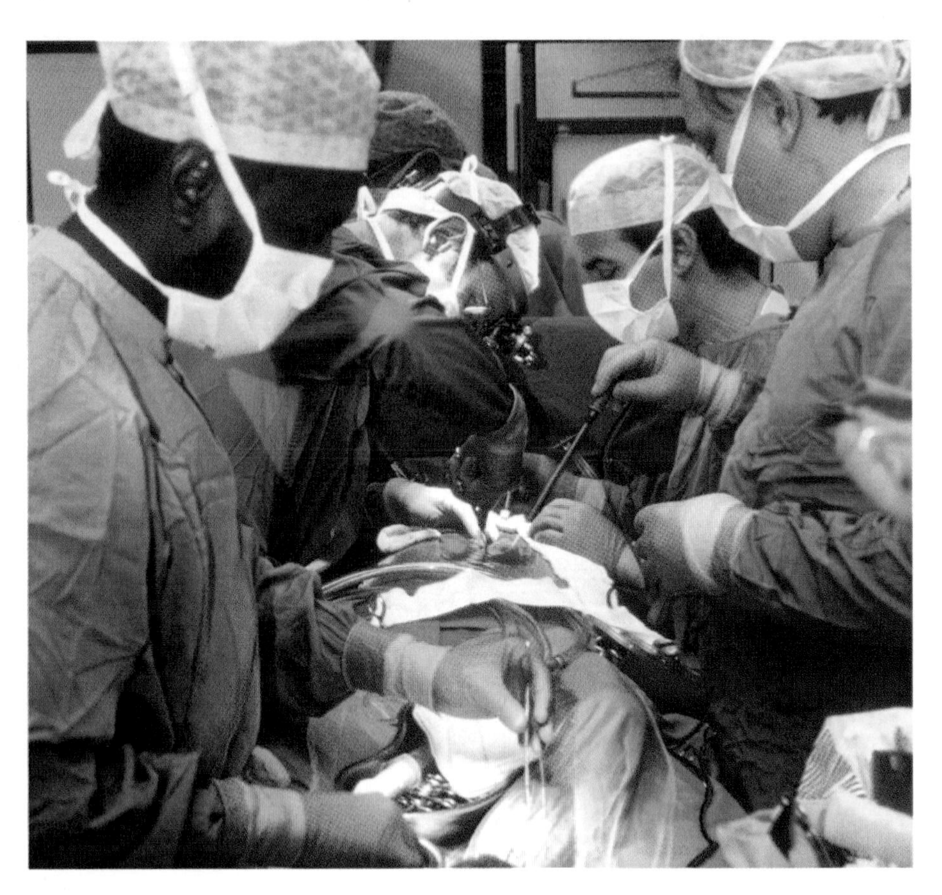

Task 10

Work in pairs. Mr Jameson's condition has worsened and his doctor has decided to refer him to a neurosurgeon. Using the cues below and the language that you have studied in this and earlier units, take turns at explaining the decision to Mr Jameson.

1 Sympathise with the patient about the continuing pain and the development of weakness in the patient's right foot.
2 Explain that this weakness is due to continued pressure on the nerve roots supplying the muscles of his leg.
3 Explain that the pressure is at the level of the disc between the lumbar vertebrae.
4 Explain that you think he should be referred to a neurosurgeon and why.
5 Reassure the patient about the operation and follow-up treatment.
6 Explain the prognosis if the patient agrees to the operation.
7 Explain the prognosis if the patient doesn't have the operation.
8 Ask the patient if there are any further points he would like explained.

When you have finished, compare your explanations with the recording.

Task 11

Study the Medications section of this Discharge Summary. Transfer this summary of the patient's medication to the Hospital Prescription Sheet on p. 84.

THE ROYAL INFIRMARY **DISCHARGE SUMMARY:**

To: Dr Winton Cardiologist Southern General Dr Wallace High Street Everton	Date of admission: 30.8.02 & 15.9.02 (SGH) Date of discharge: 5.9.02 & 24.9.02 (Memorial) Ward: 14 Consultant: Mr A. Swan

Surname: Wynne Forenames: John Number: 1563526

Address: 5 Nelson Street, Everton

Principal diagnosis: Crescendo angina ? recent myocardial infarct	Principal operation: CABG X 4, single saph grafts to LAD, RCA, sequential saph graft to OM1 and OM2
Other conditions:	Date of operation: 17.9.02 Other operations

External cause of injury

PM/no PM	Tumour type	Histological verification of tumour type	Verified/Not verified

HISTORY: 58-year-old car salesman who has been hypertensive for 15 years. Had an inferior myocardial infarction in 1998. For the past 3 months he has had increasing angina pectoris which has been present at rest. Recently admitted to hospital with prolonged chest pain, found to have positive thallium scan despite negative acute ECG or enzyme changes. Other past history of hypothyroidism diagnosed 3 years ago. Stopped smoking 20 cigarettes a day 5 years ago.

MEDICATIONS: Aspirin 300 mg daily, heparin sodium 5000 units t.d.s., diamorphine 5 mg 4 hourly p.r.n., cyclizine 50 mg 4 hourly p.r.n., paracetamol 1 g q.d.s.,
temazepam 20 mg nocte, GTN pump spray 400–800 µg p.r.n., atenolol mg daily, isosorbide mononitrate m/r 60 mg in the morning, thyroxine 0.1 mg daily, bendrofluazide 2.5 mg tablet daily, amlodipine 5 mg in the morning.

EXAMINATION: Obese. Pulse 60 regular, BP 130/80, no signs of failure, heart sounds normal. Soft midsystolic murmur at apex and aortic areas.

INVESTIGATIONS: Routine haematology and biochemistry normal. Chest X-ray: normal. ECG showed evidence of previous infarct, Q waves in T_3 + AVF, inverted T_5 in $V_1 - V_5$.

Sheet No. .... *Please use a ball point pen*

PRESCRIPTION SHEET

ORAL and OTHER NON-PARENTERAL MEDICINES – REGULAR PRESCRIPTIONS

CODE	Date Com-menced	MEDICINES (*Block Letters*)	DOSE	Method of Admin.	Times of Administration AM 6	AM 8	AM 10	MD 12	PM 2	PM 6	PM 10	MN 12	Other Times		DOCTOR'S SIGNATURE	Discontinued Date	initials
A																	
B																	
C																	
D																	
E																	
F																	
G																	
H																	
I																	
J																	
K																	
L																	

PARENTERAL MEDICINES – REGULAR PRESCRIPTIONS

CODE																	
M																	
N																	
O																	
P																	
Q																	

PLEASE ✔ WHEN MEDICINES ARE PRESCRIBED ON

Fluid (Additive Medicine) Prescription Chart	
Diabetic Chart	
Anticoagulant Chart	
Anaesthetic Prescription Sheet	
Record of Labour Sheet	

If medicine discontinued because of suspected adverse reaction please enter in box below

MEDICINE	ADVERSE REACTION
1	
2	

DIET

Date	DETAILS	Initials

ORAL and OTHER NON-PARENTERAL MEDICINES – ONCE ONLY PRESCRIPTIONS

Date	MEDICINE	DOSE	Method of Admin.	Time of Admin.*	DOCTOR'S SIGNATURE	Given by Initials	Time if Diff.*

PARENTERAL MEDICINES – ONCE ONLY PRESCRIPTIONS

Date	MEDICINE	DOSE	Method of Admin.	Time of Admin.*	DOCTOR'S SIGNATURE	Given by Initials	Time if Diff.*

	NAME OF PATIENT	AGE	UNIT NUMBER	CONSULTANT	KNOWN DRUG/MEDICINE SENSITIVITY	

Study this extract from the Procedure section. It is taken from page 2 of the Discharge Summary. Complete the gaps in the procedure using these verbs. The verbs are not in the correct order.

administered	grafted
anastomosed	opened
continued	prepared
cross-clamped	rewarmed

PROCEDURE: Vein was .... (1) for use as grafts. Systemic heparin was .... (2) and bypass established, the left ventricle was vented, the aorta was .... (3) and cold cardioplegic arrest of the heart obtained. Topical cooling was .... (4) for the duration of the aortic cross clamp.

Attention was first turned to the first and second obtuse marginal branches of the circumflex coronary artery. The first obtuse marginal was intramuscular with proximal artheroma. It admitted a 1.5 mm occluder and was .... (5) with saphenous sequential grafts, side to side using continuous 6/0 special prolene which was used for all subsequent distal anastomoses. The end of this saphenous graft was recurved and .... (6) to the second obtuse marginal around a 1.75 mm occluder.

The left anterior descending was .... (7) in its distal half and accepted a 1.5 mm occluder around which it was grafted with a single length of long saphenous vein.

Lastly, the right coronary artery was opened at the crux and again grafted with a single length of saphenous vein around a 1.5 mm occluder whilst the circulation was .... (8).

Complete Task 13 before you check your answers in the Key.

Put these steps in the correct sequence to show how the operation was completed. Step 1 is (a) and step 7 is (g). The other steps are out of sequence.

a) Release aortic cross clamp and vent air from the left heart and ascending aorta.

b) Administer protamine sulphate and adjust blood volume.

c) Defibrillate the heart and wean heart off bypass.

d) Remove cannulae and repair cannulation and vent sites.

e) Complete proximal vein anastomoses to the ascending aorta.

f) Ascertain haemostasis.

g) Insert drains.

When you have ordered them correctly, write your own version of the final section of the procedure notes like this:

– *The aortic cross clamp was released and air vented from the left heart and ascending aorta.*

Check your answers to this task and Task 12 using page 2 of the Discharge Summary in the Key on p.128.

Task 14

Using page 2 of the Discharge Summary in the Key (on p. 128), work out the meaning of these abbreviations.

1 CABG

2 LAD

3 RCA

4 OM1

5 LV

Task 15

Work in pairs. Student A should start.

A: Play the part of the surgeon. Explain to the patient in simple terms the purpose of this operation and how you will accomplish it.

B: Play the part of the patient. Ask about any points you do not understand.

When you have finished, compare your explanation with the recording.

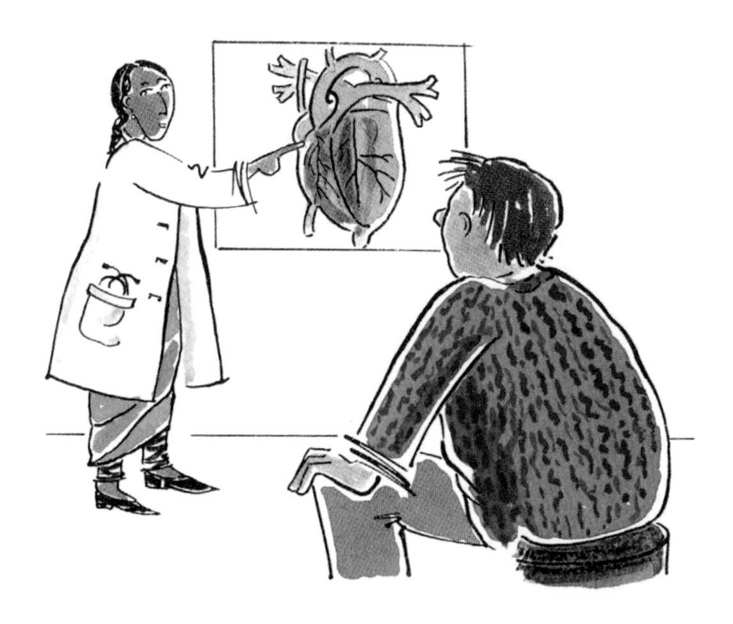

Section 4 Reading skills: Using an online database

Introduction

Medline is the largest biomedical database online. It is produced by the US National Library of Medicine (NLM). It provides bibliographic citations and author abstracts from more than 4000 publications of which around 87% are in English. New entries are made within one or two weeks of publication. It is used by health professionals and researchers worldwide.

The easiest way to access Medline is through PubMed, NLM's own interface.

http://www.ncbi.nlm.nih.gov/PubMed/medline.html

PubMed provides an online tutorial offering help on all aspects of searching Medline.

Preparing a search

You want to find out how effective arnica or cannabis is in the control of pain following surgery.

To find the information you want quickly, you need to develop an effective search strategy. This involves:

1 Posing the search question.
2 Identifying the main topics.
3 Deciding how to search for the main topics.
4 Formulating the search query.

1 Posing the search question.

In this example, the search question is:
How effective is arnica or cannabis in the control of pain following surgery?

2 Identifying the main topics.

In this case, the main topics are:
arnica, cannabis, pain following surgery

3 Deciding how to search for the main topics.

PubMed uses a standard set of NLM terms when searching the Medline database. These are known as Medical Subject Headings, MeSH. For example:
neural pathways
vascular headaches
analgesics
digestive system diseases

US spelling is used, e.g. *edema*, but UK spelling is recognised.

MeSH terms are arranged in a hierarchical manner. For example:

head
- *ear*
- *face*
  - *cheek*
  - *chin*
  - *eye*
    - *eyebrows*
    - *eyelids*
      - *eyelashes*

PubMed automatically searches for all subheadings when you enter a MeSH term.

If you enter a freetext term such as 'heart attack', PubMed will try to match this to a MeSH term (*myocardial infarction*) but it is better to use the controlled vocabulary of MeSH as this will retrieve a higher proportion of relevant articles.

Arnica and *cannabis* are both MeSH terms. The MeSH term for *pain following surgery* is *pain, postoperative*.

You can check how PubMed matches your search terms with the controlled vocabulary of MeSH by clicking on *Details*.

Task 16 Find the MeSH terms for each of the freetext terms in Column A. Some have been done for you as examples.

A *Freetext*	B *MeSH term*
1 drug	pharmaceutical preparations
2 treatment	
3 baldness	
4 limb	extremities
5 stroke	
6 heart attack	
7 bleeding nose	
8 athlete's foot	
9 boils	
10 blood poisoning	
11 cancer	
12 miscarriage	

4 Formulating the search query.

Like most databases, Medline allows you to combine your keywords using AND, OR and NOT and to 'nest' topics using brackets ( ) so the search query becomes:

(*arnica* OR *cannabis*) AND *pain, postoperative*

You can also refine your search by selecting appropriate *limits*, e.g. publication dates, publication type, age group, gender, etc., using the pull-down menus.

e.g. *pregnancy* NOT *childbirth*

Note that PubMed uses lower case except for the commands.

Task 17 Formulate search queries for each of these questions. Try them using PubMed.

1 What is the most effective treatment for cluster headaches?
2 What is the incidence of lung cancer among non-smoking men?
3 What is the most effective treatment for nasal boils?
4 What evidence is there of neurological damage among sheep farmers using organophosphorous pesticides?
5 What is the risk of disease from birds, excluding pigeons?
6 What evidence is there of asbestosis among workers in shipyards?
7 What are the risks of breast cancer associated with hormone replacement therapy using oestrogen rather than oestrogen–progestogen?
8 Is there any relationship between tattoos and hepatitis?
9 Is there any evidence of a link between marijuana use and memory loss?
10 How effective are statins in the reduction of blood cholesterol levels?

Selecting the best results

Your search results will be displayed initially in brief as shown. You can tick the citations for which you wish to see abstracts. You can click *Related Articles* to find comparable citations.

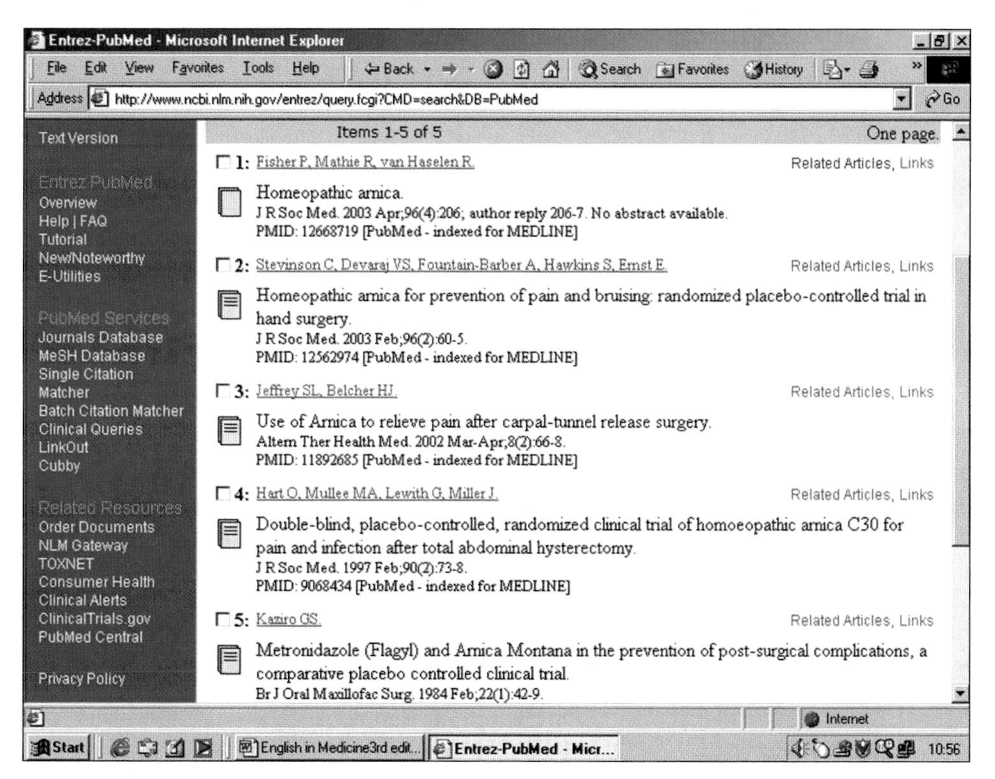

Task 18 Match these abstracts to the citations shown in the screen display on p. 89.

A

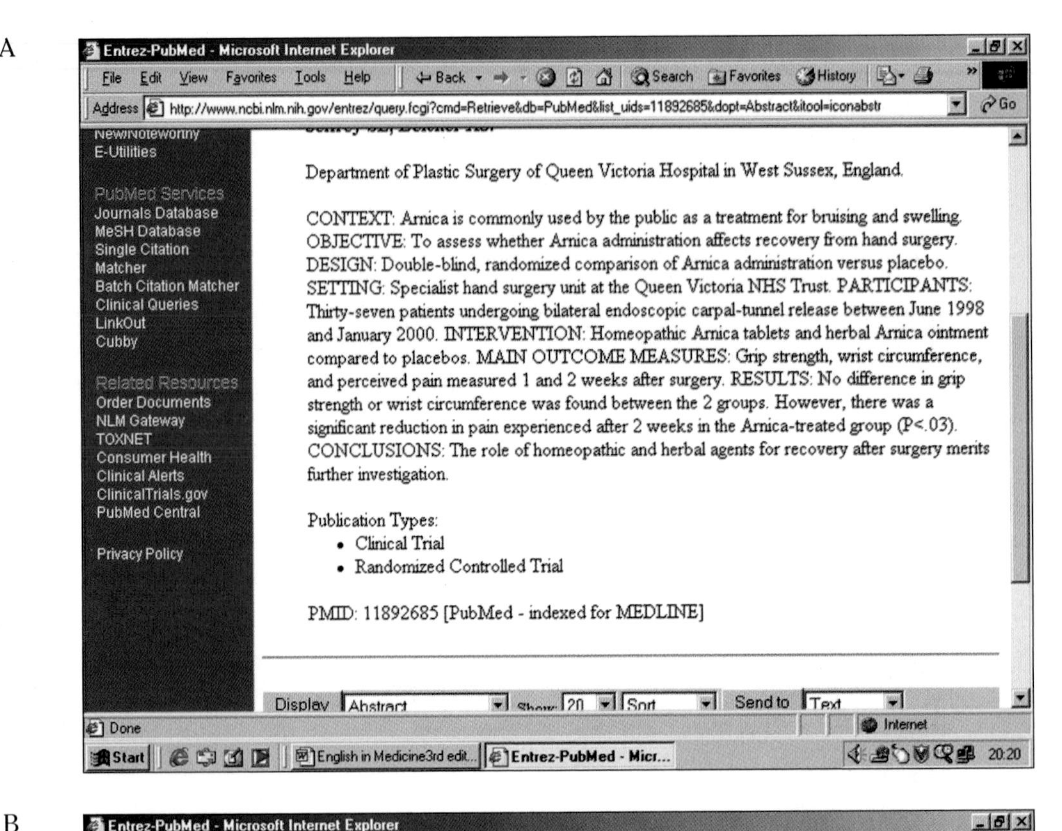
Entrez-PubMed - Microsoft Internet Explorer

Address http://www.ncbi.nlm.nih.gov/entrez/query.fcgi?cmd=Retrieve&db=PubMed&list_uids=11892685&dopt=Abstract&itool=iconabstr

Department of Plastic Surgery of Queen Victoria Hospital in West Sussex, England.

CONTEXT: Arnica is commonly used by the public as a treatment for bruising and swelling. OBJECTIVE: To assess whether Arnica administration affects recovery from hand surgery. DESIGN: Double-blind, randomized comparison of Arnica administration versus placebo. SETTING: Specialist hand surgery unit at the Queen Victoria NHS Trust. PARTICIPANTS: Thirty-seven patients undergoing bilateral endoscopic carpal-tunnel release between June 1998 and January 2000. INTERVENTION: Homeopathic Arnica tablets and herbal Arnica ointment compared to placebos. MAIN OUTCOME MEASURES: Grip strength, wrist circumference, and perceived pain measured 1 and 2 weeks after surgery. RESULTS: No difference in grip strength or wrist circumference was found between the 2 groups. However, there was a significant reduction in pain experienced after 2 weeks in the Arnica-treated group (P<.03). CONCLUSIONS: The role of homeopathic and herbal agents for recovery after surgery merits further investigation.

Publication Types:
- Clinical Trial
- Randomized Controlled Trial

PMID: 11892685 [PubMed - indexed for MEDLINE]

B

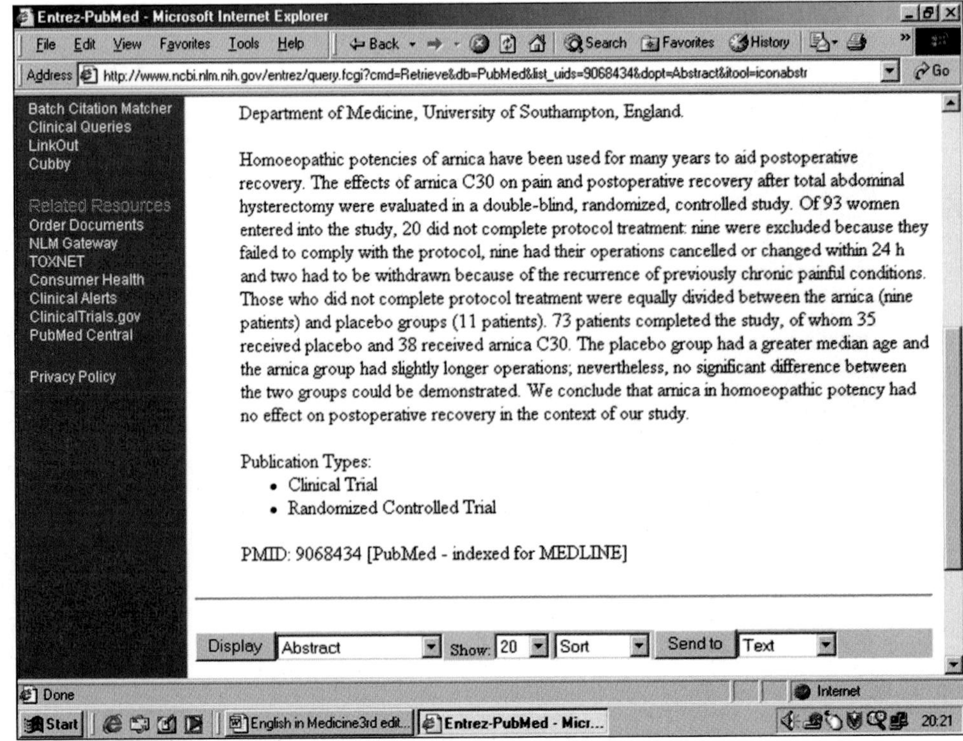
Entrez-PubMed - Microsoft Internet Explorer

Address http://www.ncbi.nlm.nih.gov/entrez/query.fcgi?cmd=Retrieve&db=PubMed&list_uids=9068434&dopt=Abstract&itool=iconabstr

Department of Medicine, University of Southampton, England.

Homoeopathic potencies of arnica have been used for many years to aid postoperative recovery. The effects of arnica C30 on pain and postoperative recovery after total abdominal hysterectomy were evaluated in a double-blind, randomized, controlled study. Of 93 women entered into the study, 20 did not complete protocol treatment: nine were excluded because they failed to comply with the protocol, nine had their operations cancelled or changed within 24 h and two had to be withdrawn because of the recurrence of previously chronic painful conditions. Those who did not complete protocol treatment were equally divided between the arnica (nine patients) and placebo groups (11 patients). 73 patients completed the study, of whom 35 received placebo and 38 received arnica C30. The placebo group had a greater median age and the arnica group had slightly longer operations; nevertheless, no significant difference between the two groups could be demonstrated. We conclude that arnica in homoeopathic potency had no effect on postoperative recovery in the context of our study.

Publication Types:
- Clinical Trial
- Randomized Controlled Trial

PMID: 9068434 [PubMed - indexed for MEDLINE]

C

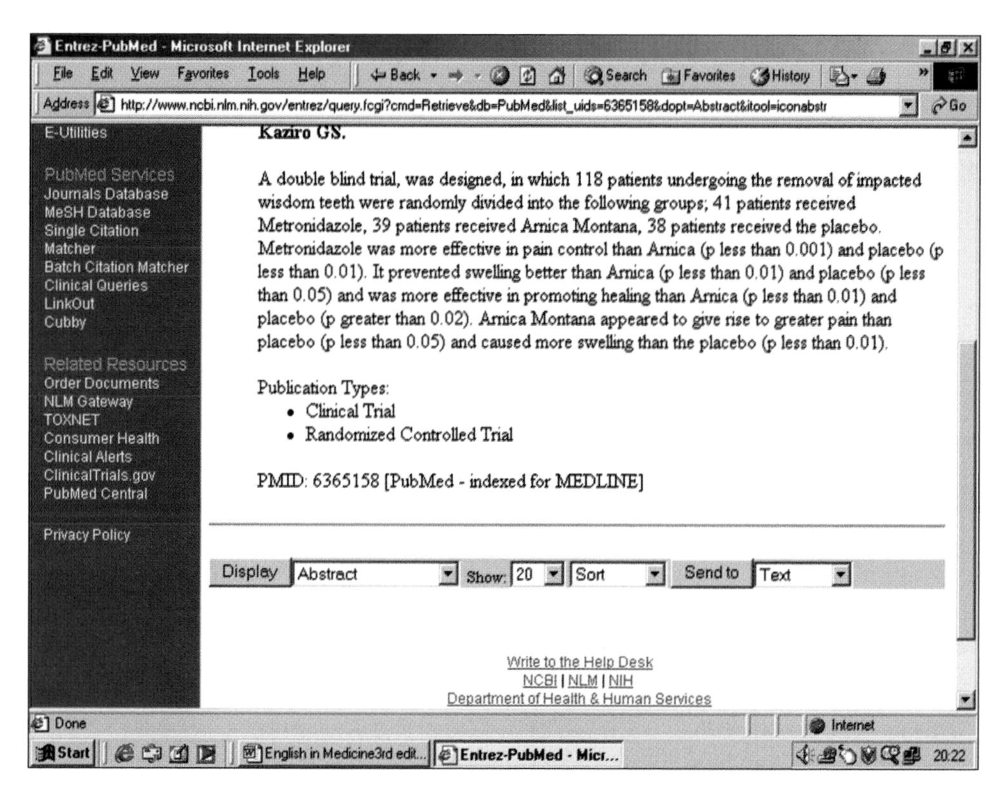

Entrez-PubMed - Microsoft Internet Explorer

File Edit View Favorites Tools Help | Back | Search | Favorites | History

Address http://www.ncbi.nlm.nih.gov/entrez/query.fcgi?cmd=Retrieve&db=PubMed&list_uids=6365158&dopt=Abstract&itool=iconabstr | Go

E-Utilities

PubMed Services
Journals Database
MeSH Database
Single Citation Matcher
Batch Citation Matcher
Clinical Queries
LinkOut
Cubby

Related Resources
Order Documents
NLM Gateway
TOXNET
Consumer Health
Clinical Alerts
ClinicalTrials.gov
PubMed Central

Privacy Policy

Kaziro GS.

A double blind trial, was designed, in which 118 patients undergoing the removal of impacted wisdom teeth were randomly divided into the following groups; 41 patients received Metronidazole, 39 patients received Arnica Montana, 38 patients received the placebo. Metronidazole was more effective in pain control than Arnica (p less than 0.001) and placebo (p less than 0.01). It prevented swelling better than Arnica (p less than 0.01) and placebo (p less than 0.05) and was more effective in promoting healing than Arnica (p less than 0.01) and placebo (p greater than 0.02). Arnica Montana appeared to give rise to greater pain than placebo (p less than 0.05) and caused more swelling than the placebo (p less than 0.01).

Publication Types:
- Clinical Trial
- Randomized Controlled Trial

PMID: 6365158 [PubMed - indexed for MEDLINE]

Display Abstract | Show: 20 | Sort | Send to Text

Write to the Help Desk
NCBI | NLM | NIH
Department of Health & Human Services

Done | Internet

Start | English in Medicine3rd edit... | Entrez-PubMed - Micr... | 20:22

D

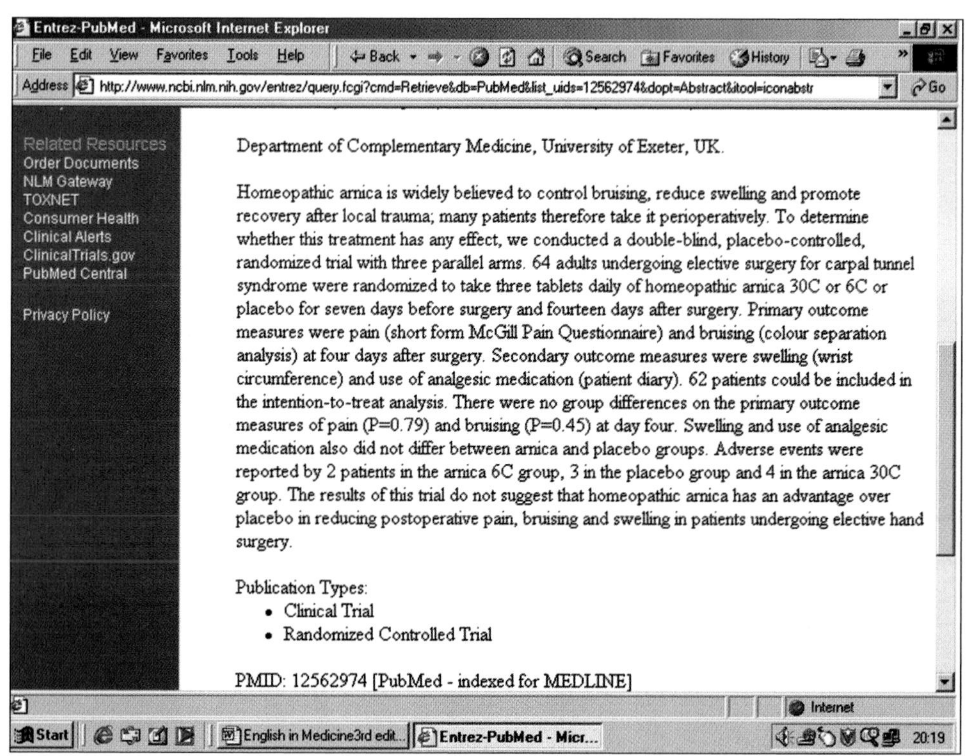

Entrez-PubMed - Microsoft Internet Explorer

File Edit View Favorites Tools Help | Back | Search | Favorites | History

Address http://www.ncbi.nlm.nih.gov/entrez/query.fcgi?cmd=Retrieve&db=PubMed&list_uids=12562974&dopt=Abstract&itool=iconabstr | Go

Related Resources
Order Documents
NLM Gateway
TOXNET
Consumer Health
Clinical Alerts
ClinicalTrials.gov
PubMed Central

Privacy Policy

Department of Complementary Medicine, University of Exeter, UK.

Homeopathic arnica is widely believed to control bruising, reduce swelling and promote recovery after local trauma; many patients therefore take it perioperatively. To determine whether this treatment has any effect, we conducted a double-blind, placebo-controlled, randomized trial with three parallel arms. 64 adults undergoing elective surgery for carpal tunnel syndrome were randomized to take three tablets daily of homeopathic arnica 30C or 6C or placebo for seven days before surgery and fourteen days after surgery. Primary outcome measures were pain (short form McGill Pain Questionnaire) and bruising (colour separation analysis) at four days after surgery. Secondary outcome measures were swelling (wrist circumference) and use of analgesic medication (patient diary). 62 patients could be included in the intention-to-treat analysis. There were no group differences on the primary outcome measures of pain (P=0.79) and bruising (P=0.45) at day four. Swelling and use of analgesic medication also did not differ between arnica and placebo groups. Adverse events were reported by 2 patients in the arnica 6C group, 3 in the placebo group and 4 in the arnica 30C group. The results of this trial do not suggest that homeopathic arnica has an advantage over placebo in reducing postoperative pain, bruising and swelling in patients undergoing elective hand surgery.

Publication Types:
- Clinical Trial
- Randomized Controlled Trial

PMID: 12562974 [PubMed - indexed for MEDLINE]

Internet

Start | English in Medicine3rd edit... | Entrez-PubMed - Micr... | 20:19

Tapescript

Unit 1 Taking a history 1

Task 1

DOCTOR: Good morning, Mr Hall. What's brought you along today?

PATIENT: Well, you see, doctor, I've been having these headaches, you see, and ...

DOCTOR: Aha, and how long have they been bothering you?

PATIENT: Er, well, they started about, well it must have been about three months ago.

DOCTOR: I see. And which part of your head is affected?

PATIENT: Well, it's, it's right across the front here.

DOCTOR: Mm. And can you describe the pain?

PATIENT: Erm, it's a sort of dull, dull and throbbing kind of pain.

DOCTOR: I see, and do they come on at any particular time?

PATIENT: They seem to be, they're usually worse in the morning. I notice them when I wake up.

DOCTOR: Mm. And is there anything that makes them better?

PATIENT: Well, if I lie down for a while, they seem to get, they go away.

DOCTOR: Yes, and has there been anything else apart from these headaches?

PATIENT: Well, the wife, my wife, she says that I seem to be getting a bit deaf.

DOCTOR: Oh? Well, Mr Hall, I think at this stage I'll start by checking your ears to see if there's any wax ...

Task 8

DOCTOR: Come in, Mr Green. Come and sit down here. I've had a letter from your doctor and she tells me that you've been having pain, pain in your chest.

PATIENT: Yes, and in my arm, and also tingling in my fingers and ...

DOCTOR: Yes, now when did you first notice this pain?

PATIENT: Er, well, I suppose about six months ago.

DOCTOR: And can you remember when it first came on?

PATIENT: Yes, well I remember, I got a bad pain in my chest when I was shopping. It was so bad I couldn't breathe and ...

DOCTOR: And where, in which part of your chest did you feel the pain?

PATIENT: Well, right across my chest.

DOCTOR: And how long did it last?

PATIENT: Ooh, about ten minutes.

DOCTOR: And what did you do when it happened?

PATIENT: I had to stop and wait for it to go away.

DOCTOR: So, have you had this, the pain again since then?

PATIENT: Yes, I often get it when I overdo things, and when I ...

DOCTOR: Well, I think at this stage I'd like to examine you, your chest. So if you could strip to your waist.

PATIENT: Right. There we go.

DOCTOR: That's fine. I'll just check your pulse first of all. Fine. That's fine. It's quite normal, seventy per minute.

PATIENT: Er, right.

DOCTOR: Now your blood pressure. Fine. That's quite normal too. 130 over 80.

PATIENT: Oh, I'm pleased to hear it.

DOCTOR: Now I'm going to listen to your heart, so I want you to breathe normally ... Mm, your heart sounds quite normal.

PATIENT: Well, that's a relief.

DOCTOR: Well now, I want you to take deep breaths in and out while I check your lungs. In. Out. In. Out. Fine. They're completely clear. Well, Mr Green, the pain you've been having sounds very much like the pain of what we call angina, and this, well, this occurs when not enough oxygen is getting to the heart. Now I'd like to check a few tests, and, following that I'll be able to advise some treatment for you ...

Task 12

DOCTOR: Ah good morning, Mr Hudson. I see from your card that you've just moved into the area and perhaps you could tell me a little about your previous health as I won't get your records for another month, month or two, and then we can deal with your present problem.

PATIENT: Well, I've actually, I've always been very fit up till now but ...

DOCTOR: Have you ever been in hospital?

PATIENT: Oh, only when I was a child. I had an appendicitis when I was eight.
DOCTOR: Aha, and what's your job, what do you do?
PATIENT: Well, I'm a, I work for the post office. I'm a postmaster.
DOCTOR: And I see that you're what, 58, now, and have you ...?
PATIENT: Yes.
DOCTOR: Have you always been with the post office?
PATIENT: Yes, well apart from my time in the army you know ...
DOCTOR: I see. And you're married. Any family?
PATIENT: Yes, two girls and a boy.
DOCTOR: Fine. That's fine. Now can you tell me what seems to be the problem today?
PATIENT: Well, it's this terrible pain. I've got this terrible pain in my back. I've had it for more than a week now and it's ...
DOCTOR: I see, and can you show me exactly where it is?
PATIENT: It's down here, here.
DOCTOR: And does it go anywhere else?
PATIENT: Yes, it goes down my left leg. And I feel pins and needles in my foot.
DOCTOR: I see, and is it there all the time?
PATIENT: Yes, yes it is. It's keeping me awake, awake at night and I can't get out into the garden. I've been taking aspirins but the pain, it just comes back again.
DOCTOR: And was there anything that started it off?
PATIENT: Well, yes, yes. I've been trying to sort out the garden at my new house and I don't know, I may have been overdoing things a bit.

Unit 2 Taking a history 2

Tasks 1 and 2

DOCTOR: Now, Mrs Brown, can you tell me, have you any trouble with your stomach or bowels?
PATIENT: Well, I sometimes get a bit of indigestion.
DOCTOR: I see, and could you tell me more about that?
PATIENT: Well, it only comes on if I have a hot, something spicy, you know, like a curry.
DOCTOR: I see, well that's quite normal really. And what's your appetite like?
PATIENT: Not bad.
DOCTOR: And any problems with your waterworks?
PATIENT: No, they're, they're all right.
DOCTOR: And are you still having your periods regularly?
PATIENT: No, they stopped, must have been five years ago.
DOCTOR: Any pain in the chest, any palpitation, swelling of the ankles?
PATIENT: Not really, doctor.
DOCTOR: And what about coughs or wheezing or shortness of breath?
PATIENT: Only when I've got a cold.
DOCTOR: Have you noticed any weakness or tingling in your limbs?
PATIENT: No, no I can't say that I have, really.
DOCTOR: What sort of mood have you been in recently?
PATIENT: I've been feeling a bit down. You know, I'm not sleeping well.

Tasks 5 and 6 and Language focus 5

DOCTOR: And how long, how long have you had this temperature?
PATIENT: Oh, I don't know exactly. About two months on and off.
DOCTOR: And does, is the temperature there all the time or does it come on at any particular time?
PATIENT: Well, sometimes I'm all right during the day but, I wake up at night and I'm drenched in sweat, drenched, and sometimes my whole body shakes and ...
DOCTOR: And how have you been feeling in general?
PATIENT: Well, I don't know, I've been feeling a bit tired, a bit tired and weak. And I just don't seem to have any energy.
DOCTOR: And have you noticed any, any pain in your muscles?
PATIENT: Yes, well, actually I have a bit, yes.
DOCTOR: And what about your weight? Have you lost any weight?
PATIENT: Yes, yes, I have, about a stone.*
DOCTOR: I see, and what about your appetite? What's your appetite been like?
PATIENT: Well, I've really been off my food this last while. I just haven't felt like eating.
DOCTOR: And have you had a cough at all?
PATIENT: Oh yes, I have. Nearly all the time. I sometimes bring up a lot of phlegm.
DOCTOR: And is there, have you noticed any blood in it?
PATIENT: No, not always but yes, sometimes.
DOCTOR: Have you had any pains in your chest?
PATIENT: Only if I take a deep breath.

---

*In the UK patients often talk about their weight in stones.
1 stone = 14 pounds or 6.4 kg.
1 pound = 454 grams.
In the USA people give their weight in pounds.

Tasks 15 and 16

GP: Hello, Jim. I wonder if you could see a patient for me?
CONSULTANT: Certainly, John. What's the story?
GP: Well, it's a Mr Alan Jameson, a 53-year-old carpenter. He's been an infrequent attender in the past but he came to see me this morning complaining of pain in his right leg and in his back.
CONSULTANT: And when did this start?
GP: Well, it came on about six weeks ago and it's become gradually more severe over the past couple of weeks.
CONSULTANT: Was the pain localised?
GP: No, poorly. At first he thought he'd just pulled a muscle. But it's got so bad that he hasn't been able to do his work properly. It's also been getting to the stage where the pain is waking him up at night, it's been so severe, and he's also noticed some tingling in his right foot. He's having difficulty in carrying on with his work. He's also lost three kilos and has become quite depressed.
CONSULTANT: Has he had anything similar in the past ?
GP: No, not exactly, but he has suffered from intermittent pain in back. Paracetamol gave some relief but didn't solve the problem completely.
CONSULTANT: Apart from that, any other problems with health in the past?
GP: No, perfectly OK.
CONSULTANT: Did you find anything else on examination?
GP: Yes, as well as the pain he has numbness in his toes on the right foot.

Tasks 19 and 20

DOCTOR: Good afternoon, Mr Hudson. Just have a seat. I haven't seen you for a good long time. What's brought you along here today?
PATIENT: Well, doctor. I've been having these headaches and I seem to have lost some weight and ...
DOCTOR: I see, and how long have these headaches been bothering you?
PATIENT: Well, I don't know. For quite a while now. The wife passed away you know, about four months ago. And I've been feeling down since then.
DOCTOR: And which part of your head is affected?
PATIENT: Just here. Just here on the top. It feels as if there were something heavy, a heavy weight pressing down on me.
DOCTOR: I see, and have they affected your vision at all?
PATIENT: No, no I wouldn't say so.
DOCTOR: Not even seeing lights or black spots?
PATIENT: No, nothing like that.
DOCTOR: And they haven't made you feel sick at all?
PATIENT: No.
DOCTOR: Now, you told me that you've lost some weight. What's your appetite been like?
PATIENT: Well, actually I haven't really been feeling like eating. I've really been off my food for the moment and ...
DOCTOR: And what about your bowels, any problems?
PATIENT: No, no they're, I'm quite all right, no problems.
DOCTOR: And what about your waterworks?
PATIENT: Well, I've been having trouble getting started and I have to, I seem to have to get up during the night, two or three times at night.
DOCTOR: And has this come on recently?
PATIENT: Well, no, not exactly. I think I've noticed it gradually over the past, the past few months.
DOCTOR: And do you get any pain when you're passing water?
PATIENT: No, no.
DOCTOR: And have you noticed any blood, any traces of blood?
PATIENT: No, no, I can't say that I have.

Unit 3 Examining a patient

Task 1

DOCTOR: Would you slip off your top things, please. Now I just want to see you standing. Hands by your side. You're sticking that hip out a little bit, aren't you?
PATIENT: Yes, well, I can't straighten up easily.
DOCTOR: Could you bend down as far as you can with your knees straight and stop when you've had enough.
PATIENT: Oh, that's the limit.
DOCTOR: Not very far, is it? Stand up again. Now I would like you to lean backwards. That's not much either. Now stand up straight again. Now first of all, I would like you to slide your right hand down the right side of your thigh. See how far you can go. That's fine. Now do the same thing on the opposite side. Fine. Now just come back to standing straight. Now keep your feet together just as they are. Keep your knees firm. Now try and turn both

shoulders round to the right. Look right round. Keep your knees and feet steady.

PATIENT: Oh, that's sore.

DOCTOR: Go back to the centre again. Now try the same thing and go round to the left side. Fine. Now back to the centre. That's fine. Now would you like to get onto the couch and lie on your face? I'm just going to try and find out where the sore spot is.

Tasks 2 and 3

DOCTOR: Would you like to lie down here on the couch, on your back?

PATIENT: OK.

DOCTOR: I'm going to test your reflexes by tapping you with this little hammer. It won't hurt you. Let me hold your right arm. Let it go quite relaxed. Try not to tighten up. There. Now the other one. Just let me have your wrist. Let it go quite floppy. That's right. I'm going to tap your elbow. Fine. Now the left one. OK?

PATIENT: Fine.

DOCTOR: I'll just give you a little tap here on the wrist. Now the other one. Now let your legs go completely relaxed. I'll hold them up with my hand. There. I'm just going to turn your leg out to the side for a moment. Just relax. That's it. Now the other one. Fine.

Task 4

1

Firstly I'd like you to kneel on that straight-backed chair so that your feet are just slightly hanging over the edge. That's right. Now I'm going to tap them behind your heel with this hammer. This is just a method of testing for your ankle jerk. That's fine.

2

Now I'd like you to sit with your legs just dangling over the edge of the couch so that I can test your knee jerks. Now nothing very much is happening here, so what I'd like you to do is to clasp your hands together with the fingers and try to pull your fingers apart. Pull as hard as you can and concentrate on pulling. That's fine. That makes it a lot easier to produce your knee jerk.

3

Now finally I want you to lie down on the bed with your legs stretched out in front of you. Now I'm going to place my hand on your knee and with this key I'm going to stroke the sole of your foot to see which way your big toe will turn. This is called the plantar reflex. You shouldn't find it painful although it may tickle a little. Fine. Now I'll check the other foot. Very good. That's your reflexes all finished now. Thank you.

Task 5

DOCTOR: Would you like to get onto the couch and lie on your back, please? Now I'm going to take your left leg and see how far we can raise it. Keep the knee straight. Does that hurt at all?

PATIENT: Yes, just a little. Just slightly.

DOCTOR: Can I do the same with this leg? How far will this one go? Not very far. Now let's see what happens if I bend your toes back.

PATIENT: Oh, that's worse.

DOCTOR: I'm going to bend your knee. How does that feel?

PATIENT: A little better.

DOCTOR: Now let's see what happens when we straighten your leg again.

PATIENT: That's sore.

DOCTOR: I'm just going to press behind your knee.

PATIENT: Oh, that hurts a lot.

DOCTOR: Where does it hurt?

PATIENT: In my back.

DOCTOR: Right. Now would you roll over onto your tummy? Bend your right knee. How does that feel?

PATIENT: It's a little bit sore.

DOCTOR: Now I'm going to lift your thigh off the couch.

PATIENT: Oh, that really hurts.

Task 6 and Language focus 7

DOCTOR: Now, Mr McLeod, I know you're in some pain but there are a few things I'll have to check. I'll be as quick as I can. I'll just take your pulse. Mm. Now the other side. OK. Now your blood pressure. You've had that done before. I'm going to check the other side too. Once more. Fine. Now I want to listen to your heart. Just breathe normally. Could you sit up a little? I just want to check your lungs.

PATIENT: Right, doctor.

DOCTOR: That's it. Now I'd like you to take big breaths in and out through your mouth. OK. You can lie down again.

PATIENT: It's bad.

DOCTOR: I'll be quick. I'll just take a look at your stomach. Take deep breaths in and out. Now I'm going to check the pulses in your groins too. We'll just roll your pyjama trousers down. That's it. We're finished now. Well Mr McLeod, I think you've got some trouble with one of your arteries because of your high blood pressure. I'll give you an injection to relieve the pain and arrange for you to go into hospital for further tests.

Task 10

DOCTOR: How are you, Mrs Wallace?
PATIENT: I'm fine.
DOCTOR: Have you brought your urine sample?
PATIENT: Yes, here it is.
DOCTOR: I'll just check it. Fine, just slip off your coat ... Urine is all clear. Now if you'd like to lie down on the couch, I'll take a look at the baby. I'll just measure to see what height it is. Right. The baby seems slightly small.
PATIENT: How do you know that?
DOCTOR: I measure from the top of your womb to your pubic bone. The number of centimetres is roughly equal to the number of weeks you're pregnant. In your case it's 29 centimetres but you're 32 weeks pregnant.
PATIENT: Why do you think the baby's small?
DOCTOR: It might be because your dates are wrong. Remember you weren't sure of your last period. The best thing would be to have another scan done. I'll make an appointment for you next week.
PATIENT: Which way round is the baby lying?
DOCTOR: The baby's in the right position. It's coming head first. Now I'm going to listen for the baby's heartbeat. That's fine. Can you hear it? It's quite clear. Have you noticed any swelling of your ankles?
PATIENT: Not really.
DOCTOR: Let's have a quick look. No, they seem to be all right. Now, would you like to sit up and I'll take your blood pressure.
PATIENT: Right.
DOCTOR: It's quite normal. Now I'll take a sample of blood to check your haemoglobin. Fine. You can get your shoes and coat on again now.

Task 13

DOCTOR: I'll just check a few things to see if we can get to the bottom of these problems. First of all I'll check your pulse and then I'll do your blood pressure. I'd like you to take off your jacket and roll up your sleeve.
PATIENT: How is it doctor?
DOCTOR: It's just a little above normal, but that doesn't mean too much. If you'd like to roll up your shirt, I'm going to check your heart and lungs. Now just breathe normally. Good. Now I'd like you to take deep breaths in and out through your mouth. That's fine. Now if you'd like to lie down on the couch, I'll examine your stomach.
PATIENT: Right.
DOCTOR: Take a deep breath in and out. And again. Aha. Now I'll just see if there's any sign of a hernia. Could you slip your trousers down? That's fine. Give a cough, please. Again, please. Now because you've been having trouble with your waterworks, I'd like to examine your back passage. If you'd roll over on to your left side and bend your knees up. You might find this a bit uncomfortable, but it won't take long. That's it. All finished. You can get your clothes on now.

Unit 4 Special examinations

Tasks 1, 2 and 3

DOCTOR: Good afternoon, Mr Priestly, come in and have a seat.
PATIENT: Good afternoon, Mr Davidson.
DOCTOR: Now I've had a letter from your doctor saying that you've been having problems with your sight.
PATIENT: Yes, that's right doctor.
DOCTOR: Could you tell me how long the left eye has been bad for?
PATIENT: Oh, going on for about a year now, I suppose.
DOCTOR: Mm, and what do you do?
PATIENT: I'm a postman. I deliver letters and that sort of thing.
DOCTOR: How is your work being affected?
PATIENT: Oh, it's really bad. I can hardly see the letters let alone the addresses. I have to get my mates to do that sort of thing for me and it's getting to a stage where I just can't cope really.
DOCTOR: I see, yes. I'd just like to examine your eyes and perhaps we could start with the chart. Could you just look at the chart for me? Can you see any letters at all?
PATIENT: No, nothing.
DOCTOR: OK. Well, with the right eye can you see anything?
PATIENT: N H T A. That's about all, I'm afraid.
DOCTOR: Now does that make any difference?
PATIENT: No, no nothing.
DOCTOR: What about that one? Does that have any effect?
PATIENT: Not really, I can't really say it does.
DOCTOR: Right, OK, thank you very much indeed.

Tasks 7 and 8

DOCTOR: Now, Debbie, can I have a look at you to find out where your bad cough is coming from?
PATIENT: *(Nods)*
DOCTOR: Would you like to stay sitting on Mum's knee?

PATIENT: *(Nods)*

DOCTOR: That's fine. Now let's ask Mum to take off your jumper and blouse. You'll not be cold in here. *(Mother removes Debbie's clothes)* Now I'm going to put this thing on your chest. It's called a stethoscope. It might be a bit cold. I'll warm it up. Feel the end there. OK? First of all I listen to your front and then your back.

MOTHER: She's had that done lots of times by Dr Stuart.

DOCTOR: Good, well done, you didn't move at all. Now I'd like to see your tummy, so will you lie on the bed for a minute? Will I guess what's in your tummy this morning? I bet it's Rice Krispies.

PATIENT: *(Nods)*

DOCTOR: Now while you're lying there, I'll feel your neck and under your arms. Are you tickly? Now the top of your legs. That's all very quick, isn't it? Mrs Thomson, could Debbie sit on your knee again? I'd like you to hold her there while I examine her ears and throat. Right, Debbie. Here's a little light to look in your ears. This will tickle a bit but won't be sore. Good girl. What a nice ear. Now let's see the other one. Now nearly the last bit. Open your mouth. Let me see your teeth. Now open it as wide as you can. Good. I wonder how tall you are, Debbie. Could you come and stand over here and I'll measure you? Stand straight. That's fine. Have you ever been on a weighing machine? Just stand up here and we'll see how heavy you are. Well, we're all finished now. You've been very good. I'll have a talk with your Mum and you can play with the toys for a minute.

Task 9

5 *Foot*

DOCTOR: We'll just ask Mummy to take off your shoes and socks so I can have a quick look at your feet. It might be tickly but it won't be sore.

6 *Nasal passage*

DOCTOR: Can you sit on Mummy's knee? I'm going to have a look at your nose with this little light. You won't feel anything at all. Can you put your head back to help me?

Tasks 11, 12, 13 and 14

DOCTOR: Hello, Mr Walters. How are you today?

PATIENT: Oh, I'm fine, very well, thank you.

DOCTOR: You know who I am, don't you?

PATIENT: Now, let me see now. I know your face, but I can't quite place who you are. I think I know. I think I should know who you are.

DOCTOR: Well, that's right. I'm Dr Williams. I've met you several times before, you know.

PATIENT: Oh, you're the doctor. Well, I remember old Dr Horsburgh quite well. I remember when he had a surgery down in the old Kirkgate, but I don't remember seeing him recently.

DOCTOR: No, Dr Horsburgh's been retired for a good number of years now. I took over his practice and I've seen you before. Maybe you don't recall that. Have you been here long?

PATIENT: Where, where do you mean?

DOCTOR: In this house, have you been here long?

PATIENT: Oh, I've been here some time I think.

DOCTOR: Do you remember where this is? Where is this place?

PATIENT: This'll be the High Street, isn't it?

DOCTOR: Yes, this is the High Street. How long have you been living in the High Street?

PATIENT: Oh, it must be a good number of years now. I, my mother used to stay down in North High Street of course, and I used to stay with her, but when I got married I moved up here. Oh, that must be a good number of years. I can't quite remember the time.

DOCTOR: Do you remember when you were born? What was the year of your birth? Can you remember that?

PATIENT: Oh, yes. I was born in 1913.

DOCTOR: Oh, what month were you born in? Do you remember that?

PATIENT: Oh, yes. I'm an April baby. I was always an April baby. Not an April fool, not the 1st of April you know.

DOCTOR: Do you remember what time of the month? What was the date?

PATIENT: Oh, it was the 17th of April.

DOCTOR: Well, how old will you be now, do you think?

PATIENT: Oh, I've retired now. I must be about 69, I think. I'll be about 69.

DOCTOR: Well, there's no doubt the years go by. What year is it this year? Do you know that?

PATIENT: Well, this'll be about 1989 now, I suppose.

DOCTOR: Fine, and what month are we in?

PATIENT: Oh, now let me see. It'll be, the, I can't, can't remember, doctor.

DOCTOR: Well, tell me, is it summer or winter?

PATIENT: Oh, well I suppose it's so cold it must be the winter time. It'll be January. Is that right?

DOCTOR: Well, actually it's February now, but it feels as though it was January, doesn't it?

Do you remember what day of the week it is? Or do the days not mean a great deal to you now that you're not working?

PATIENT: Oh, you're right the days seem to run into each other, but this'll be Tuesday, I think. No, no it'll be Wednesday, isn't it?

DOCTOR: Well, I suppose that Wednesday or Thursday, one day tends to become much the same as the other when we're not working. Isn't that right?

PATIENT: Oh, you're right there.

Task 16 and Language focus 11

Part 1

DOCTOR: I now want to test how well you can feel things on the skin. I'm going to ask you to close your eyes and say 'yes' each time you feel me touching the skin of your legs with this small piece of cotton wool.

PATIENT: Uhuh.

DOCTOR: I'll touch the back of your hand with it now. Do you feel that?

PATIENT: Yes, doctor.

DOCTOR: Well every time you feel me touch your legs say 'yes'.

Part 2

DOCTOR: Well, that was quite easy, wasn't it? Now I'm going to try something a little different. I have this sharp needle with this blunt end. I want you to say 'sharp' or 'blunt' each time you feel me touch.

Part 3

DOCTOR: The other sensation I want to test is whether you feel this tube hot or this other tube which is cold. Remember I want you to keep your eyes closed, and each time I touch the skin of your legs I want you to tell me whether it's hot or cold.

PATIENT: Right.

Part 4

DOCTOR: Next I'm going to test you with this vibrating fork. I'm going to press it on the ankle bone and I want you to tell me whether you feel it vibrating, and if you do, to say 'stop' when you feel it's stopped.

Task 18

Part 5

DOCTOR: I'm now going to test the pulses in your legs. First we'll press on the blood vessel here in the groin. And now behind the knee. Could you bend it a little for me?

PATIENT: Mm, sorry.

DOCTOR: And here behind the ankle bone. And now at the top of the foot. And now the other leg.

Unit 5 Investigations

Task 2

DOCTOR: Now I'm going to take some fluid off your back to find out what's giving you these headaches. Nurse will help me. It won't take very long. Now I want you to move right to the edge of the bed. That's it. Right. Lie on your left side. Right. Now can you bend both your knees up as far as they'll go? That's great. I'll just put a pillow between your knees to keep you comfortable. There you go. Put your head right down to meet your knees. Curl up. Now I'm going to wipe your back with some antiseptic. You'll feel it a bit cold, I'm afraid. Now I'm going to give you a local anaesthetic so it won't be sore. You'll feel just a slight jab, OK? There. We'll wait for a few minutes for that to take effect. Right now, lie still, that's very important.

Task 4

1 *ECG*

DOCTOR: Your pulse is a bit irregular. I'm not quite certain why this is but I think we'll have to get a tracing of your heartbeat. I want you to strip down to the waist and also take off your shoes and socks. First of all, this is a completely painless procedure. Are you quite comfortable? It's better if you're as relaxed as possible before I start to take the cardiograph. It only takes a few minutes to do the actual test but it takes a bit longer to get you wired up. I'm just putting some cream on your wrists and ankles. That's everything ready. Now just relax as much as you can.

2 *Barium meal*

DOCTOR: Good morning, Miss Jones. This test is to help me get a picture of the inside of your gullet and your stomach so that we can find out what's causing you these pains there. I want you just to stand here while I give you a cup of liquid to drink. This liquid will show up after you've drunk it and will be able to tell me if you have an ulcer in your stomach or duodenum. I'd like you to drink the liquid now and I'll be taking pictures of it as it goes down. That's fine. Thank you.

3 *Crosby capsule*

DOCTOR: Now I'm just going to give you a little jab to help your tummy relax. Just a little prick. OK? That's fine. Good girl. Now I want you to open your mouth for me so that I can pass this little tube down into your tummy. That's fine. Good girl. Nothing to worry about. Head back a little. That's fine. Now can you swallow for me? And again? Good girl. Now I want you to try and keep as still as possible.

4 *Ultrasound scan*

DOCTOR: I'd like you to lie down on this table here. This gel helps to get a contact so that the picture is clear. We'll just rub in the gel a little bit and now I'll put on the equipment. Try to keep as still as you possibly can. That's good. Now if you turn your head to the left, you'll be able to see the scan as I'm taking it. As you see, it's just like a television picture. This black part here is the baby's head and this is the body. As you can see, it's moving around very well. These dots allow me to measure the baby so we can work out when your baby is due ... That's everything finished now.

5 *Myelogram*

DOCTOR: We're going to put a little needle in your back. We'll inject some fluid in, put you onto the table there and take some X-ray pictures. These will help us to know exactly where the trouble is. Now roll onto your left side. That's it. I want you to roll up into a little ball, to bring your knees up and tuck your head down. That's fine. Now I'm going to swab your back. You'll feel it a bit cold. Now you'll feel me pressing on your back. All right? Scratch coming up now. Now you'll feel me pressing in. OK. That's fine. I'm just injecting the stuff in. You shouldn't feel it at all. That's it. OK. I'll just take the needle out now. Now just straighten out gently and lie on your front. We'll take the pictures now.

Task 5

DOCTOR 1: An ECG is essential because it will show any changes in the heart: axis, ischaemia, left ventricular hypertrophy.

DOCTOR 2: I think a chest X-ray is also very important to see the heart and the extent of the hypertrophy. I would also check the creatinine to see if there's any damage to the kidneys.

DOCTOR 3: An intravenous pyelogram is essential because a renal cause is very likely.

DOCTOR 2: As an initial investigation?

DOCTOR 3: No, after urea and electrolytes and after the creatinine.

DOCTOR 2: It's essential *if* the creatinine shows something wrong with the kidneys.

DOCTOR 3: Yes.

DOCTOR 1: Yes, both creatinine and urea and electrolytes are required. In this case I think they're more important than the ECG and chest X-ray because the patient is young, 43, and the hypertension is very high.

DOCTOR 3: Urinalysis too in this case. It's very important.

DOCTOR 2: Yes, it's routine.

DOCTOR 3: We can see if there's any glomerular damage. We may find blood, albumen, casts ...

DOCTOR 1: Yes, it's very important.

DOCTOR 2: What about radioisotope studies of the kidneys?

DOCTOR 3: Not essential, but we could do this to check the function of the kidneys.

DOCTOR 1: We can see that from the creatinine and urine.

DOCTOR 3: I know. It's not essential, but it could be useful.

DOCTOR 2: Serum cholesterol?

DOCTOR 1: Not essential. We're thinking of another type of hypertension here. But possibly useful.

DOCTOR 2: MRI scan of the brain?

DOCTOR 3: Not required. It's of no value in this case.

DOCTOR 2: Serum thyroxine?

DOCTOR 1: Absolutely no connection with hypertension.

DOCTOR 2: Barium meal?

DOCTOR 3: Not required.

DOCTOR 2: Uric acid?

DOCTOR 1: Not necessary. If the uric acid is raised, there would be other symptoms.

Task 7

1 *Mr Gumley*

DOCTOR: Mr Gumley, you'll have to have some investigations done to find out exactly what's causing your problem. Firstly we need to get your chest X-rayed. Then for three mornings running I'd like you to bring to the surgery a sample of the phlegm that you cough up in the morning. We'll be sending that off to the lab for testing to see if you have any particular germs present. Following that, it'll be necessary for you to have a bronchoscopy done. This is an investigation which involves looking down into your lungs through a tube. We'll have to admit you to hospital for the day to do it. It's not a particularly pleasant investigation but you'll be given an anaesthetic spray before the tube is passed down into your lungs. Usually it doesn't take more than a few minutes but it may last longer if they need to take samples of the tissue in your lungs – maybe up to 20 minutes. You have to take this test with an empty stomach, so you won't have any breakfast that day. You'll be able to get home again after the test, but you'll have to wait until the anaesthetic has worn off before you eat anything.

2 *Mrs Emma Sharp*

DOCTOR: Because of your heavy periods, Mrs Sharp, we must find out if you've become anaemic so I'll have to take a blood test.

PATIENT: Oh, right.

DOCTOR: I think it will also be necessary for you to have a D&C done in hospital. We can probably do this as a day case. It's a very simple procedure and just involves removing a small piece of the lining from inside the womb to find out why your periods have become so heavy. It will also give us a better chance to examine you under the anaesthetic. It might also be necessary to do a pelvic ultrasonograph. This is a very simple test which takes a special picture of the lower end of your abdomen to see if the womb is enlarged.

3 *Miss Grace Donaldson*

DOCTOR: From your symptoms it would seem that you have an overactive thyroid gland. We can test this quite simply by doing a blood test to check the level of hormones in your blood.

4 *Mr Pritt*

DOCTOR: Because you've been having this trouble with abdominal pain after fatty foods I think you may have some stones in your gall bladder. You'll need to have a special X-ray done. This is called a cholecystogram, and it will involve you taking some tablets before attending the X-ray department. They'll take an ordinary X-ray first and then give you something fatty to eat. After which they'll take pictures of the gall bladder area to see if your gall bladder is working properly and if there are any stones present. They may also do an ultrasonograph. This is a way of examining your abdomen using a special machine which can show us pictures of your stomach and gall bladder using sound signals. It's not painful at all and it doesn't take more than five or ten minutes to perform.

5 *Barry Scott*

DOCTOR: Mrs Scott, I feel certain that Barry has German measles. Sometimes we do a blood test to prove this definitely, but because he's only two and a half, I'm sure he wouldn't like to have a blood test done and it would be safer to do nothing.

6 *Mrs Mary Lock*

DOCTOR: Mrs Lock, I think it's possible that you have a condition called glaucoma which is caused by increased pressure inside the eye. In order to prove this it will be necessary for you to have the pressure inside your eyes measured. We use a small instrument with a scale on it to measure the pressure. We'll put a few drops of local anaesthetic on your eye so you shouldn't feel anything. The test only takes a few seconds.

Task 8

LAB TECH: This is the haematology lab at the Royal. I have a result for you.

DOCTOR: Right, I'll just get a form. OK.

LAB TECH: It's for Mr Hall, Mr Kevin Hall.

DOCTOR: Right.

LAB TECH: White blood cells, seven point two; RBC, three point three two; haemoglobin, twelve point nine. That's twelve point nine. Haematocrit, point three nine; MCV, eighty-one; platelets, two six four.

DOCTOR: Sorry?

LAB TECH: Two six four, two hundred and sixty-four.

DOCTOR: Right.

LAB TECH: ESR, forty-three millimetres.

DOCTOR: OK. I've got that.

LAB TECH: Blood film showed: neutrophils, sixty per cent; lymphocytes, thirty per cent; monocytes, five per cent; eosinophils, four per cent; basophils, one per cent.

DOCTOR: Fine. Anything else on the film?

LAB TECH: Yes, there are burr cells present – plus plus.

DOCTOR: Right. Thanks very much.

Task 16

CONSULTANT: Your father's condition is quite poor. It seems that he's had diarrhoea for six days and this may have affected his diabetes. As you know, any infection can cause diabetes to get out of control. First we have to check his blood sugar, kidney function and level of salts. Because he's very dehydrated we'll also be giving him some fluid. He'll have an X-ray done of his chest and abdomen. Lastly we'll be checking to see which particular germ caused his diarrhoea.

Unit 6 Making a diagnosis

Tasks 1 and 2

DOCTOR: Hello, Mr Nicol, I haven't seen you for a long time. What seems to be the problem?
PATIENT: I've been having these headaches, doctor.
DOCTOR: Which part of your head?
PATIENT: Mostly along here, along the side.
DOCTOR: Oh, I see, the left side. How long have they been bothering you?
PATIENT: Well, they started about three weeks ago. At first I felt as if I had the flu because my shoulders were aching, you know, pains in the joints and I had a bit of a temperature.
DOCTOR: I see, and did you take anything for the headaches?
PATIENT: I took some aspirin but it didn't seem to make much difference to me.
DOCTOR: When do they come on?
PATIENT: They seem to be there all day long, and at night I just can't get to sleep.
DOCTOR: So they're bad enough to keep you awake?
PATIENT: Yes.
DOCTOR: And how do you feel in yourself?
PATIENT: Very weak, and I'm tired of course. I think I've lost some weight.
DOCTOR: Have you had headaches in the past?
PATIENT: Just one or two, but never anything like this.

Task 7

DOCTOR: Well, Mr Jameson, there's a nerve running behind your knee and your hip and through your spine.
PATIENT: Uhuh.
DOCTOR: When you lift your leg, that nerve should slide in and out of your spine quite freely, but with your leg, the nerve won't slide very far. When you lift it, the nerve gets trapped and it's very sore. When I bend your knee, that takes the tension off and eases the pain. If we straighten it, the nerve goes taut and it's painful.
PATIENT: Aye.
DOCTOR: Now what is trapping the nerve? Well, your MRI scan confirms that you've got a damaged disc in the lower part of your back.
PATIENT: Oh, I see.
DOCTOR: The disc is a little pad of gristle which lies between the bones in your spine. Now, if you lift heavy loads in the wrong way, you can damage it. And that's what's happened to you. You've damaged a disc. It's pressing on a nerve in your spine so that it can't slide freely and that's the cause of these pains you've been having.
PATIENT: Uhuh.
DOCTOR: Now we're going to try to solve the problem first of all with a maximum of twenty-four hours' bed rest and with strong painkillers so that you'll be able to get moving again as soon as possible. Bed rest for too long can make things worse. We'll also give you some physio to ease your leg and back. I can't promise this will be entirely successful and we may have to consider an operation at a later date.

Task 10

1 *A 33-year-old salesman suffering from a duodenal ulcer*
DOCTOR: Your stomach has been producing too much acid. This has inflamed an area in your bowel. It's possible that your stressful job has aggravated the situation. This is quite a common condition and there is an effective treatment. It doesn't involve surgery.

2 *A 6-year-old boy with Perthes' disease, accompanied by his parents*
DOCTOR: What's happened to your son's hip is caused by a disturbance of the blood supply to the growing bone. This causes the bone to soften. When he walks, it puts pressure on the bone and it changes shape. It's painful and he limps. This problem isn't uncommon with young boys and if we treat it now, it won't cause any permanent damage.

3 *A 21-year-old professional footballer with a torn meniscus of the right knee*
DOCTOR: The cartilage, which is the cushioning tissue between the bones of your knee, has torn when your knee was twisting.
PATIENT: Right.
DOCTOR: We need to do some further tests – an MRI scan and possibly an arthroscopy.
PATIENT: Sorry ...

DOCTOR: That means looking into the joint with a kind of telescope. If there is torn cartilage, we can remove it then. Footballers often get this kind of problem and with treatment and physio, you will be able to play again.

PATIENT: Oh, right.

4 *A 43-year-old teacher with fibroids*

DOCTOR: Er, well your heavy periods are caused by a condition known as fibroids. Fibroids are a type of growth in the womb.They're not related to cancer and they're quite common. When you get to the change of life, they may become smaller and cause you no trouble but at your age and because the bleeding has made you anaemic, the best treatment is an operation.

5 *An 82-year-old retired nurse suffering from dementia, accompanied by her son and daughter*

DOCTOR: Your mother is in the early stages of dementia which is a condition of the brain in older people which causes loss of memory, particularly recent memory. Sometimes people with dementia also have delusions. Her personality may change, for example she may become rude or aggressive. Her mood may become very up and down. At this stage she can stay at home with some help but her condition will deteriorate and she will need to go into care in the long term.

6 *A 2-week-old baby with tetralogy of Fallot, accompanied by her parents*

DOCTOR: Your baby has a heart condition which developed when she was growing in the womb. Some babies with this condition are born looking blue but it's also possible for the blueness to develop after a few weeks. The blood flow in the heart becomes abnormal and this causes your baby to grunt and have difficulty in feeding. Fortunately there is an operation for this condition which is very successful. It's extremely likely your baby will go on to lead a normal life.

7 *A 35-year-old receptionist suffering from hypothyroidism*

DOCTOR: The cause of your problem is your thyroid gland which is situated here in your neck. The hormones from this gland affect all areas of your body. If the gland isn't working properly, many things can go wrong. For example, it can cause weight gain and hair loss. This is a common condition and the treatment is simple.

PATIENT: Good.

Task 13

SURGEON: We've operated on your father and discovered that he'd had a blockage of the blood supply to his small bowel. This caused the small bowel to become gangrenous and it had to be removed. He'll be able to manage without it but it is a fairly major operation and naturally his condition is serious. The blockage of blood supply caused his diarrhoea and because of the diarrhoea his diabetes went out of control as he lost so much fluid and salts from his body. That explains why he went into a coma.

Unit 7 Treatment

Task 2

PATIENT: Do I have to rest completely? I really just want painkillers so I can get back to work.

DOCTOR: Because the pain is so bad at the moment, you should rest for a day or two but it's really not good to rest for longer than that. Your back is designed for movement so you must stay active to keep healthy. If you rest for a long time, your muscles will get weaker and the pain will feel worse. I'll give you painkillers so you can soon become active again. Take them every six hours. Don't wait until the pain is out of control. And I'll refer you to physiotherapy for advice on specific exercises.

PATIENT: Will I need to be off work?

DOCTOR: You'll need a few days off work because of the job you do but we'll get you back to work as soon as possible.

Task 3

1 *A hypertensive 50-year-old director of a small company*

DOCTOR: The condition you have requires to be controlled to prevent future damage to the body, especially the blood vessels. If it's not controlled, you can have certain serious illnesses such as a heart attack or a stroke. Treatment is therefore to prevent illness developing because I'm sure that you don't feel ill at the moment. You'll have to take tablets, or medicine, but you'll also have to modify some of your habits. For instance, you must stop smoking.

2 *An insulin-dependent 11-year-old girl accompanied by her parents*

DOCTOR: Now Elizabeth, the trouble with you is that you're not making a substance that you need to control the amount of sugar in your blood. If you have too much sugar or too little sugar, it'll make you feel very ill and we'll have to replace this each day. It means that you'll have to have a jab because it doesn't work properly if we give it to you in a tablet. Now your mother here will go with you to see the nurse and she'll show you how to do it. Many other boys and girls, some much younger than you, soon learn to do it, so you needn't feel frightened.

3 *A 65-year-old schoolteacher with osteoarthritis of the left hip*

DOCTOR: This condition is really like the wear and tear of a hinge. The joint is becoming stiff and painful because it's roughened by inflammation. Fortunately, as you're now retired, you'll be able to modify your life so that it doesn't trouble you so much. I'll prescribe tablets which will help the pain and stiffness and, although this won't cure it, it will control the discomfort.

PATIENT: Right.

DOCTOR: If, in the future, it gets more troublesome, we can always consider an operation which will get rid of the pain.

4 *A 23-year-old sales representative affected by epilepsy*

DOCTOR: Unfortunately, the attacks you've been having are shown to be quite severe. They're caused by abnormal electrical activity in your brain. This is called epilepsy. But we can help you to stop having these fits. I'll prescribe tablets for you. These will control the condition as long as you're taking them.

PATIENT: Right.

DOCTOR: Now it's most important that you take them regularly and don't forget. The problem as far as you're concerned is that you're not permitted to drive for at least one year after your last attack. You'll have to consider changing your job. You must tell your employer about your condition.

5 *A 52-year-old cook with carcinoma of the bowel*

DOCTOR: The tests show that you've got a nasty growth in the bowel which will have to be removed. It's far too dangerous to leave it. The operation has every chance of removing the disease. The exact type of operation, however, will depend on what the surgeon finds in the operation. There's a possibility that you may have to have an opening made on the skin of your abdomen. This is something a lot of people can cope with and it may only be temporary.

6 *A 27-year-old teacher of handicapped children suffering from a depressive illness*

DOCTOR: I know that you feel this illness is something which affects your whole life. It's called depression and we think it's due to chemical changes in the brain. Now it's not something you can pull yourself out of – you'll need help in the way of psychotherapy and drugs as well. You may think that nobody else has ever felt like you're feeling, but let me assure you that this is quite a common condition. You will get well again, although it will take some weeks to feel improvement. Often it's possible to continue in your routine of work because this gives you something rewarding to do while you're getting better. You'll get a medicine to take which will take some weeks to work, so don't be more despondent if at first it doesn't seem to be helping.

7 *A 6-month-old baby boy suffering from atopic eczema, accompanied by his parents*

DOCTOR: This skin problem your baby has isn't an infection so he can't give it to anybody else. It's a condition which affects the skin and will require ointments from time to time. Sometimes it will seem better and then it may flare up again. It's not absolutely certain what causes this problem but it can be hereditary.

Task 5

DOCTOR: Now Mr Jameson, here is a prescription for some tablets which you are to take two of every six hours. Try to take them after meals if possible in case they cause you indigestion. You can take them during the night as well if you are awake with the pain.

Tasks 7, 8 and 9

PHYSIO: First of all, you lie down on your tummy on a hard surface. The floor will do. Now place your hands on your back and lift one leg up straight without bending your knee. Then bring it down and lift the other leg up in the same way and then bring it down. Repeat this exercise five times doing it alternately with each leg.

Keeping the same position, place your hands on your back and lift your chest up off the floor, and then bring it down slowly. Repeat this exercise five times.

Now keeping your hands at your sides and lying on your tummy, lift alternate leg and arm simultaneously – for example your right leg and left arm – and then bring them down. Next lift your other alternate leg and arm, and then bring them down. Repeat this exercise five times.

Keep your hands on your back and then lift your chest and legs up simultaneously, and then bring them down slowly. Repeat this exercise also five times. This is a difficult exercise but with practice you'll be able to do it properly.

Now you have to change position. So lie on your back with your hands on your sides and bend your knees up, keeping your feet on the floor. Now lift up your bottom and then bring it down slowly. Repeat this exercise five times.

You should do these exercises three times a day, preferably on an empty stomach before meals. Then depending on your progress, after two weeks or so we'll increase the number of times you do these exercises. You should try to do them as slowly and smoothly as possible and try to avoid jerking your body.

Task 10

DOCTOR: Well, Mr Jameson, I am sorry to see that your back is still causing you pain and that you have now developed a weakness in your right foot. The weakness is due to the continued pressure on the nerve roots supplying the muscles of your leg. This pressure, of course, is taking place at the level of the disc between the lumbar vertebrae. Due to this worsening of the condition, I think that there is now a strong possibility that you require an operation on the back to remove the disc where it's pressing on the nerve.

PATIENT: I see.

DOCTOR: The operation will need to be carried out by a surgeon specialised in this work, a neurosurgeon. The operation itself will only immobilise you for a few days, and you'll soon be up and about again and back to the physiotherapist to improve the strength of your muscles, both in your back and this leg. If you don't have the operation, the risk is that your right foot will be permanently weak. We want to avoid this at all costs. Are there any questions you would like to ask me?

Task 15

SURGEON: The diameter of one of your coronary arteries is reduced, so one part of your heart muscle is starved of oxygen and other nutrients. If you don't have an operation, you will continue to have pain in your chest and you may even have a further heart attack. Before serious damage is done, we must try to improve the flow of blood to the heart. We're going to remove a vein from your leg and use it to replace part of your coronary artery. The chances of recovery are very good and I'm confident you'll feel a lot more comfortable after the operation.

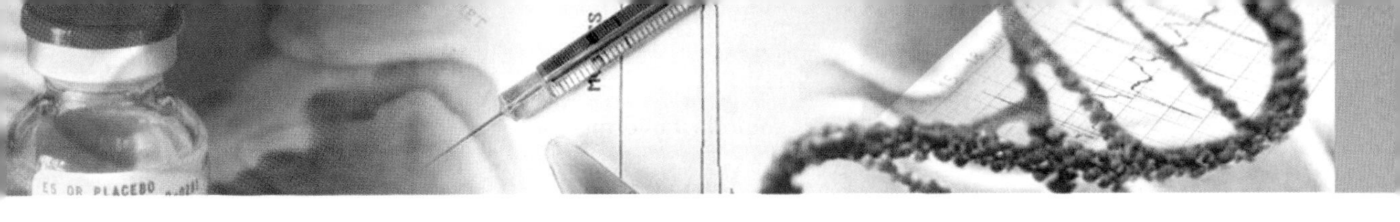

Key

Unit 1 Taking a history 1

Task 1

SURNAME *Hall*	FIRST NAMES *Kevin*
AGE *32* SEX *M*	MARITAL STATUS *M*
OCCUPATION *Lorry driver*	
PRESENT COMPLAINT *frontal headaches $^{3}/_{12}$* *worse in a.m. – "dull, throbbing"* *relieved by lying down* *also $^{c}/_{o}$ deafness*	

1 male

2 married

3 for three months (similarly 3/52 = three weeks; 3/7 = three days)

4 morning

5 They are the patient's own words.

6 complains of

Task 4 Use this diagram to tell you where to indicate in each case.

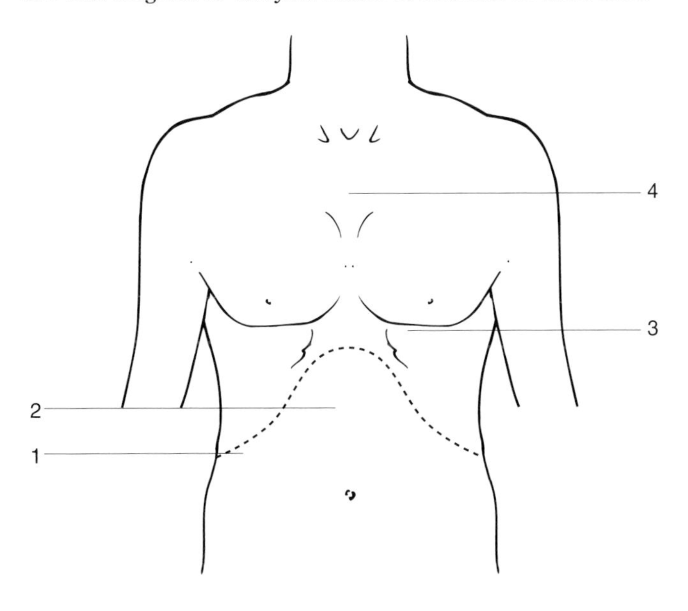

Task 5

B: Use this additional information to answer any questions the doctor asks.

1 Greasy food, like fried eggs, upsets you most. The pain lasts several hours.

2 The pain wakes you at night. Around 2 or 3 in the morning. Spicy food brings on the pain. Too much to drink also makes it worse.

3 The pain is really bad. You've been coughing up brownish spit. You've had a temperature.

4 You've had a cold. You're not coughing up phlegm.

Diagnoses

1 gall bladder

2 duodenal ulcer

3 pneumonia

4 tracheitis

Task 6

(A full list of abbreviations is given in Appendix 2.)

O/E on examination
BP blood pressure
CNS central nervous system
-ve negative
? query/possible
1/52 one week

Task 7

Suggested questions:

1 What's your occupation?
What do you do?
What's your job?

2 Whereabouts was the pain?
Show me where the pain was.

3 When did the pain first happen?

5 Did anything make it better?

6 Does anything special bring it on?

7 Are your parents alive?
How old was your father when he died?
What age did your father die at?

Task 8

1 Green

2 42

3 Salesman

4 Central

5 10 mins

6 clear/normal

7 P (pulse)

8 BP (blood pressure)

9 HS (heart sounds)

Task 9 Possible questions:

a) What's your name?
How old are you?
Are you married?
What's your job?
What's brought you here today?
Where exactly is the pain?
How long have you had it?
Did anything special bring it on?
Is it worse at any particular time?
Does anything make it better or worse?
Have you any other problems?
Have you taken anything for it?
Did the paracetamol help?

b) How long have you been suffering from these headaches?
How long do they last?
How often do you get them?
Do they ever make you feel sick?
Have you noticed any other problems?
How does the pain affect you?

Task 11

1 bus driver
2 cough and general malaise
3 lower respiratory tract infection
4 barely rousable and breathless at rest
5 severe chest infection
6 two weeks
7 myocardial infarction
8 drank little alcohol

Task 12

SURNAME Hudson		FIRST NAMES William Henry
AGE 58	SEX M	MARITAL STATUS M
OCCUPATION Postmaster		

PRESENT COMPLAINT
c/o severe low back pain. 1/52 radiating to left leg. Accompanied by parasthesia. Unable to sleep because of pain. Unrelieved by paracetamol.
May have started after gardening.

Unit 2 Taking a history 2

System	Complaint	No complaint	Order
ENT			
RS		✓	4
CVS		✓	3
GIS		✓	1
GUS		✓	2
CNS		✓	5
Psychiatric	✓		6

Task 3

1 c 2 f 3 b 4 d 5 a 6 e

Task 4

Information for Student B (patient):

1 You are a 60-year-old electrician (male).
You have coughed up blood several times over the last few weeks.
You have noticed that you're losing weight. Your clothes don't fit you properly.
You smoke 30 cigarettes a day.

2 You are 68. You are a retired schoolteacher (male).
You have been getting more and more constipated over the past few months. You've noticed blood in your stools.
You've been losing weight.

3 You are 45. You are a housewife. You have three children.
You get a pain in your stomach after meals. Sometimes you feel squeamish.
Fried and oily foods seem to be worst.

4 You are a 24-year-old typist (female).
You have pain when you are passing water. There is blood in your urine.
You have to pass water more frequently than usual.

5 You are a student of 19 (male).
You have a headache at the front of your head, along the brow.
Your nose keeps running.
Your headache is worse in the morning when you get up.
It also gets worse when you bend down.

Diagnoses

a) cancer of the colon
b) fibroids
c) cancer of the lung
d) cystitis
e) bronchitis
f) cholelithiasis
g) sinusitis

Solutions
See foot of page 110.

Tasks 5, 6 and 9

FEVER
- ✓1 duration
- frequency
- ✓2 time
- chills
- sweats
- ✓3 night sweats
- ✓4 rigor

GENERAL SYMPTOMS
- ✓5 malaise
- weakness
- ✓6 myalgia
- ✓7 wt loss
- drowsiness
- delirium
- ✓8 anorexia
- vomiting
- photophobia

bleeding?
- nose
- skin
- urine

ACHES AND PAINS
- head
- teeth
- eyes
- abdomen
- chest
- neck
- loin
- back
- pubic
- muscle
- joints
- bone

SKIN
- rash
- pruritis
- bruising

CVS
- c dyspnoea
- palpitations
- ht irregularity

GIS
- diarrhoea
- e melaena

RESPIRATORY
- ✓9 cough
- f coryza
- sore throat
- c dyspnoea
- ✓11 pleuritic pain
- sputum
- ✓10 haemoptysis

URINARY
- a dysuria
- frequency
- strangury
- discolouration

NEUROLOGICAL
- vision
- d photophobia
- blackouts
- b diplopia

Language focus 5

weight cough blood chest

Task 7

(Other questions are also possible.)

3 Does the pain come on at any particular time?

4 Apart from the pain, do you feel anything else wrong?

5 Do you smoke? How much do you smoke?

6 When did you first notice the pain?

7 Have you noticed any change in the frequency of the pain?

8 How has your weight been?

9 Do you ever become aware of your heart beating too quickly?

10 Have you had any problem with swelling of the ankles?

There are many possible orders for the questions depending on the patient's responses.

Task 10

1 k 2 c 3 f 4 j 5 l 6 d 7 i 8 b 9 a 10 e 11 g 12 h

Task 11 Information for Student A (patient):

Name: Mr Peter Wilson
Age: 48
Sex: M
Marital status: M
Occupation: Steelrope worker

You had an attack of chest pain last night. The pain was behind your breastbone. You also had an aching pain in your neck and right arm. The pain lasted for 15 minutes. You were very restless and couldn't sleep. You've also been coughing up rusty coloured spit.

For the past year you've suffered from breathlessness when you walk uphill or climb stairs. You've had a cough for some years. You often bring up phlegm. In the past three weeks on three occasions you've felt a tight pain in the middle of your chest. The pain has spread to your right arm. These pains happened when you were working in the garden. They lasted a few minutes. Your ankles feel puffy. You find that your shoes feel tight by the evening although this swelling goes away after you've had a night's rest. You've had cramp pains in your right calf for the last month whenever you walk any distance. If you rest, the pains go away.

You've been in good health in the past although you had whooping cough and wheezy bronchitis as a child. You smoke 20 to 30 cigarettes a day. Your mother is still alive, aged 80. Your father died of a heart attack when he was 56. You have one sister. She had TB when she was younger.

Task 12

1 breathlessness
2 productive
3 oedema
4 intermittent claudication
5 retrosternal/central
6 rusty

Task 13

7 short
8 dyspnoeic
9 cyanosis
10 clubbing
11 regular
12 oedema
13 some
14 venous
15 clavicular
16 heart
17 crepitations
18 right
19 IV
20 IM

Solutions to Task 4 (p.108) 1 c 2 a 3 f 4 d 5 g

Task 15

SURNAME Jameson		FIRST NAMES Alan
AGE 53	SEX M	MARITAL STATUS M
OCCUPATION Carpenter		
PRESENT COMPLAINT Acute backache referred down R sciatic nerve distribution. Began $^6/_{52}$ ago and became more severe over past $^2/_{52}$. Affecting work and waking him at night. Also $^c/_o$ tingling in R foot. Wt loss 3 kg. Depressed.		
IMMEDIATE PAST HISTORY Paracetamol helped a little with previous intermittent back pain.		

Task 16

1 What's
2 when
3 did
4 Was/Is
5 Has
6 had
7 in
8 that/this
9 other
10 with
11 in
12 Did
13 find
14 on

Task 17

(Other answers are possible.)

a) What's brought you here today?
   Where is the pain?
b) Does the pain affect your sleep?
c) Apart from the pain, have you noticed any other problems?
d) Is it affecting your work?
e) Have you noticed any change in your weight?
f) Have you ever had any problem like this before?
g) Did you take anything for it?
   Did it help?

The consultant is probably a neurologist or an orthopaedic surgeon.

Task 18

	Angina	*Pericarditis*
Site	left-sided or central chest pain	chest, retrosternal and left precordial
Radiation	neck, jaw, arms, wrists, sometimes hands	back and trapezius ridge, sometimes either or both arms
Duration	a few minutes	persistent
Precipitating factors	exertion, exposure to cold, heavy meals, intense emotion, lying flat, vivid dreams	inspiration, coughing and changes in body position
Relief of pain	rest, sublingual nitrate	sitting up and leaning forwards
Accompanying symptoms and signs	choking sensation, breathlessness, often no physical signs	pericardial friction rub

Task 19

SURNAME Hudson		FIRST NAMES William Henry
AGE 65	SEX M	MARITAL STATUS W
OCCUPATION Retired postmaster		

PRESENT COMPLAINT
Headaches for 4 mths. Wt loss. Headaches feel "like a heavy weight".
No nausea or visual symptoms.
No appetite.
Diff. starting to PU. Nocturia x3.

Task 20

On the recording the doctor does not always speak in sentences. Sometimes he stops in the middle of what he is saying, says 'um' or 'er' and repeats himself. This is typical of spoken language and gives the doctor time to think.

Unit 3 Examining a patient

Task 1

1 e 2 c 3 a 4 d 5 b 6 f

Task 2

1 d 2 b 3 e 4 a 5 c

Task 5

1 lie
2 raise/lift
3 bend
4 bend
5 straighten
6 press
7 hurt
8 roll
9 feel
10 lift/raise

Task 6

1 radial pulses
2 BP
3 heart sounds
4 lungs
5 abdomen
6 femoral pulses

Task 8

THE FIRST EXAMINATION

1 Height ☐
2 Weight* ☑
3 Auscultation of heart and lungs ☐
4 Examination of breasts and nipples ☐
5 Examination of urine ☑
6 Examination of pelvis ☐
7 Examination of legs ☑
8 Inspection of teeth ☐
9 Estimation of blood pressure ☑
10 Blood sample for blood group ☐
11 Blood sample for haemoglobin ☐
12 Blood sample for serological test for syphilis ☐
13 Blood sample for rubella antibodies ☐
14 Blood sample for HIV antibodies ☐
15 Examination of abdomen to assess size of uterus ☑
16 Examination of vagina and cervix ☐

* In the UK, weight is no longer measured as routine on subsequent visits.

a 5 b 9 c 11 d 7 e 15

Task 9

Suggested order:

1 a 2 e 3 d 4 b 5 c

Task 11

1 cefotaxime
2 benzylpenicillin, erythromycin
3 amoxicillin
4 cefuroxime
5 benzylpenicillin
6 gentamicin, benzylpenicillin
7 erythromycin, tetracycline
8 phenoxymethylpenicillin, benzylpenicillin
9 tetracycline
10 erythromycin

Task 12

PU	pass urine
?AF	possible atrial fibrillation
HS	heart sounds
abdo.	abdomen
p.r.	per rectum
NAD	no abnormality detected, nothing abnormal detected
4/12	four months
Ca.	carcinoma, cancer

Task 14

PARTICULARS OF PATIENT IN BLOCK LETTERS PLEASE

Hospital use Only	Clinic	Day Date	Time	Hospital No.	GP112

Ambulance Required Sitting/Stretcher: Yes / ~~No~~ ✓

REQUEST FOR OUT-PATIENT CONSULTATION

Urgent Appointment Required: ~~Yes~~ ✓ / No

Hospital: EASTERN GENERAL — Date: 29/4/02

Please arrange for this patient to attend the ... clinic of ~~Dr~~/Mr FIELDING

Patient's Surname: HUDSON — Maiden Surname: ...

First Names: WILLIAM HENRY — ~~Single/Married~~/Widowed/~~Other~~

Address: 14 LINDEN LEA, NORTHCOTT — Date of Birth: 30/2/37

Patient's Occupation: POSTMASTER (Retired)

Postal Code: EH21 3LH — Telephone No. ...

Has the patient attended hospital before: YES/~~NO~~? If "YES" please state:

Name of Hospital: NORTHERN GENERAL

Year of Attendance: 1980 — Hospital No. ...

If the patient's name and/or address has/have changed since then please give details:

Name, Address and Telephone Number of MEDICAL/DENTAL PRACTITIONER

DR PETER WATSON
HEALTH CENTRE
NORTHCOTT

Please use rubber stamp

I would be grateful for your opinion and advice on the above named patient. A brief outline of history, symptoms and signs is given below:

This recently retired postmaster complains of difficulty starting to pass urine and increased frequency. He has nocturia x3. Rectal examination shows moderate enlargement of the prostate. I also discovered that he has atrial fibrillation which is under treatment with digoxin 0.25 mg and warfarin. There is no cardiac enlargement and his BP is $^{160}/_{105}$. His PSA is within the normal range. This fibrillation is presumably due to ischaemic heart disease, but I feel that he would fairly soon require some surgery to the prostate and this may become urgent.

Diagnosis/provisional diagnosis: (1) Enlarged prostate (2) Ischaemic heart disease

Present drug treatment and potential special hazards: digoxin 0.25 mg, warfarin – dose variable depending on INR

Relevant X-rays available from: ... No. (if known) ...

Signature: Peter Watson

Unit 4 Special examinations

Task 1

SURNAME Priestly		FIRST NAMES John
AGE 58	SEX M	MARITAL STATUS M
OCCUPATION Postman		
PRESENT COMPLAINT Failing sight. L eye has deteriorated over past year. Seriously affecting his work – "can't cope".		

The patient has been referred to the Ophthalmology Department (the Eye Clinic).

Task 2

a) all

b) can

c) anything

d) that

e) any

f) that

g) that

(d) and (f) refer to lenses.

Task 3

1 Can you see any letters at <u>all</u>?

2 Well, with the <u>right</u> eye, can you see anything?

3 Now does <u>that</u> make any difference?

4 What about <u>that</u> one? Does <u>that</u> have any effect?

Task 4

1 d 2 c 3 b 4 f 5 a 6 e

Possible instructions:

2 I'm going to examine your ears. Could you turn your head this way?

3 I'd like to examine your chest. Could you remove your top clothing?

4 I'll just check your back. Would you stand up, please?

5 Would you like to take your shoe and sock off and I'll examine your foot.

6 If you'd like to tilt your head back, I'll just examine your nasal passage.

Task 5

1 limb power

2 lung vital capacity

3 consolidation of the lungs

4 eye movements

5 temperature

6 rectum

7 coordination of the right limb

8 throat/tonsils

Task 6 Compare your version with the Tapescript for Task 1.

Task 7 RS, GIS, glands, ENT, height and weight.
Paediatric.
The patient is a 4-year-old girl (with her mother).

Task 8

a) going
b) called
c) might
d) of
e) to
f) then
g) done
h) like
i) so
j) you're
k) I'll
l) tickly
m) Now
n) all
o) isn't

Task 9 For paediatric examination of the throat (1), ears (2), chest (3) and back (4) see the Tapescript for Task 7.

5 *foot*
We'll just ask Mummy to take off your shoes and socks so I can have a quick look at your feet. It might be tickly but it won't be sore.

6 *nasal passage*
Can you sit on Mummy's knee? I'm going to have a look at your nose with this little light. You won't feel anything at all. Can you put your head back to help me?

Tasks 10, 11 and 12

Test question	*Order*	*Patient's score*
1	1	1
2	8	0
3	7	0
4	6	0
5	5	0
6	3	1
7	4	1
8	–	–
9	2	0

Total score 3/8
= severe impairment

Task 13

1 What was the year of your birth?

2 Can you remember that?

3 What was the date?

4 How old will you be now, do you think?

5 Do you know that?

6 Well, tell me, is it summer or winter?

7/8 Or do the days not mean a great deal to you now that you're not working?

b) question 7

c) question 5

d) question 4

e) question 3

f) question 2

Task 14

1 What was the year of your <u>birth</u>?

2 Can you <u>remember</u> that?

3 What was the <u>date</u>?

4 How old will you be by <u>now</u>, do you think?

5 Do you know <u>that</u>?

6 Well, tell me, is it <u>summer</u> or <u>winter</u>?

7/8 Or do the days not mean a great <u>deal</u> to you now that you're not <u>working</u>?

Task 15

1 What is this place called?
Where are we now?

2 Which day is it today?
What day is this?

3 What is this month called?
What month are we in now?

4 What year are we in?
What is the year?

5 How old are you?
What is your age?

6 When were you born?
What was your year of birth?

7 What is your date of birth?
What month were you born in?

8 What's the time?
Can you tell me the time?

9 How many years have you been living here?
For how long have you stayed here?

Task 16

1 b 2 a 3 c 4 d

Task 20

1 Title

2 Authors

3 Editor's note

4 Summary

5 Introduction

6 Materials and methods

7 Results

8 Comment

9 References

Task 21

Title – h
Authors – a
Editor's note – e
Introduction – g
Materials and methods – b
Results – d
Comment – f
References – c

The typeface and linguistic features such as key words and tenses help identify the parts.

Task 22

1 Objective(s)

2 Methods

3 Results

4 Conclusions

Task 23

1 Objective

2 to the

3 Methods

4 of the

5 of the

6 by

7 for

8 Results

9 to the

10 of

11 than

12 nor

13 who

14 Conclusions

15 of

16 However

17 not

18 to

Task 24

Dear Dr Watson,

Your patient, Mr Hudson, was admitted as an emergency on 23 February with acute retention of urine due to his enlarged prostate for which he was awaiting elective surgery.

On admission to the ward he was still in rapid atrial fibrillation and his blood pressure was 180/120. The bladder was distended to the umbilicus and p.r. showed an enlarged soft prostate. He was sedated and catheterised. Urinalysis showed 3+ glucose and GTT showed a diabetic curve. He was therefore started on diet and metformin 500 mg t.d.s.

Dr Wilson, our physician, is dealing with the cardiac side of things before we go ahead with the operation.

Yours sincerely,

You should add to the Diagnosis section: (3) ? Diabetes.

Unit 5 Investigations

Task 1

2 your left/right side

3 knees

4 down

5 up

6 still

Task 3

1 d

2 c

3 a

4 f

5 g

6 e

7 b

Task 5

Essential	*Possibly useful*	*Not required*
chest X-ray	radioisotope studies	barium meal
creatinine	serum cholesterol	MRI scan of the brain
ECG		serum thyroxine
IVP (IVU)		uric acid
urea and electrolytes		
urinalysis		

Task 6

1 chest X-ray, bronchoscopy, sputum culture

2 pelvic ultrasound, Hb, EUA and D & C

3 serum thyroxine, TSH

4 cholecystogram, abdominal ultrasound

5 Normally no investigations are required. In a hospital situation a physician may choose to give throat swab, monospot, viral antibodies, full blood count.

6 tonometry

Task 8

TELEPHONE REPORT FROM HAEMATOLOGY LABORATORY

PATIENT'S NAME: HALL Kevin UNIT NO:

BLOOD FILM

WBC $\times 10^9$/L	7.2	NEUTRO	60 %
Hb g/dl	12.9	LYMPH	30 %
Hct	0.39	MONO	5 %
MCVfl	81	EOSINO	4 %
Platelets $\times 10^9$/L	264	BASO	1 %
ESR mm	43		

OTHER INFORMATION

RBC 3.32

burr cells ++

PROTHROMBIN RATIO .... :1

TIME MESSAGE RECEIVED .... AM/PM

MESSAGE RECEIVED BY ....

DATE RECEIVED ....

Task 9

(Other answers are possible.)

Sodium is elevated.
Potassium is raised.
Bicarbonate is low.
Plasma urea is abnormally high.

Task 10

1. complained
2. found
3. normal
4. blocker
5. diuretic
6. elevated/high/raised
7. albumen
8. 12.9
9. 43 mm
10. burr
11. greatly/very
12. 50.1
13. 16
14. chronic renal failure

Task 11

Dear Dr Chapman,

Thank you for referring this pleasant 42-year-old salesman. These episodes of central chest pain which he describes with radiation to the L arm and fingers sound very typical of angina. Physical examination was unrevealing.

I have checked various blood parameters including serum cholesterol, triglyceride and HDL cholesterol. CXR was normal but exercise ECG showed ST depression.

Serum cholesterol was elevated at 7.2 mmol/l.

I will be seeing him again next week to let him have these results. I shall arrange for him to be seen by the dietician and prescribe simvastatin 10 mg at night. In view of the family history I am sure this will be worthwhile.

Yours sincerely,

Paula Scott

Dr Paula Scott

Task 12

1 Title
2 Authors
3 Summary
4 Introduction
5 Patients and methods
6 Results
7 Discussion
8 References

Task 13

a) Title
b) Summary
c) Discussion
d) Results
e) Introduction
f) Authors
g) References

Task 14

The extract is from Patients and methods.

1 or
2 of
3 in
4 before
5 were
6 to
7 was
8 this
9 A
10 the
11 at
12 making
13 the
14 patients
15 on
16 about
17 they
18 for/to
19 by
20 all

Task 15

1 diarrhoea
2 metformin (Glucophage)
3 three
4 cardiac
5 dehydrated
6 semi-comatose
7 irregular
8 abdomen
9 tenderness
10 absent
11 possible
12 TUR – transurethral resection

Task 16

The investigations:

X-ray chest/abdomen
blood urea and electrolytes
blood sugar
stool culture

Unit 6 Making a diagnosis

Task 1

SURNAME Nicol		FIRST NAMES Harvey
AGE 59	SEX M	MARITAL STATUS M
OCCUPATION Office worker		
PRESENT COMPLAINT c/o headaches, L side for 3/52, unrelieved by aspirin. Initially flu-like symptoms. Unable to sleep. Slight weight loss. Feels "weak and tired".		

Task 2

(Other answers are possible.)

space-occupying lesion
migraine
viral fever
aneurysm
temporal arteritis
depression
cervical spondylosis

Task 3

temporal arteritis
migraine
depression

unlikely – space-occupying lesion, viral fever, aneurysm
excluded – cervical spondylosis

Investigations – full blood count and ESR
– MRI scan
– superficial left temporal artery biopsy

Task 4 Raised ESR and polymorphs strongly indicate and the biopsy confirms that the patient has temporal cell arteritis.
Normal MRI scan excludes space-occupying lesion.

Task 5

1 nephrotic syndrome
2 Henoch-Schonlein syndrome
3 mononucleosis, glandular fever
4 cholelithiasis
5 scleroderma

Task 7

1 explanation of cause
2 proposed treatment
3 warning of possible operation

Task 8

1 The pancreas is a gland near the stomach which helps digestion and also makes insulin.
2 The thyroid is a gland in the neck which controls the rate at which your body works.
3 Fibroids are growths in the womb which are not cancerous but cause heavy bleeding.
4 Emphysema is a condition in which the structure of the lung is destroyed and makes breathing difficult.
5 An arrhythmia is an irregularity of the heartbeat, for example when you have an extra beat.
6 Bone marrow is where the various types of blood cells are made.
7 The prostate gland produces some of the secretions which mix with semen. Sometimes it becomes enlarged and causes trouble in passing water.
8 This is what happens when acid from your stomach comes back up into the gullet. It causes heartburn.

Task 9

1 If the stomach produces too much acid, it may cause stomach pain.
2 If a woman gets German measles during pregnancy, the baby may be born with deformities.
3 If you vomit several times in quick succession, you may burst a blood vessel in the gullet.
4 If your skin is in contact with certain plants, you can develop dermatitis.
5 If your blood pressure remains high, you may have a stroke.
6 If you give your baby too much fruit, he or she will get diarrhoea.
7 If the cholesterol level in the blood gets too high, you may have a heart attack.
8 If there are repeated injuries to a joint, it may develop arthritic changes.

Task 11

a) Summary

b) Discussion

c) Results

d) Introduction

e) Authors' affiliations

f) References

The title of the article is 'Gender differences in general practitioners at work'.

Task 12

1 in
2 were
3 about
4 of
5 of
6 of
7 of
8 about
9 about
10 were
11 who
12 for
13 out
14 about
15 from
16 with
17 with
18 of
19 were
20 of
21 on
22 were
23 the
24 were
25 were
26 of
27 for
28 in
29 but
30 of
31 was
32 were
33 was
34 when
35 were
36 for
37 of
38 were
39 a

Tasks 1 and 2

SURNAME Jameson FIRST NAMES Alan

AGE 53 SEX M MARITAL STATUS M

OCCUPATION Carpenter

PRESENT COMPLAINT
Acute backache referred down R sciatic nerve distribution.
Began $^{6}/_{52}$ ago and became more severe over past $^{2}/_{52}$.
Affecting work and waking him at night. Also $^{c}/_{o}$ tingling in
R foot. Wt loss 3 kg. Depressed.

O/E
General Condition Fit, well-muscled.

ENT NAD

RS NAD

CVS Normal pulsations at femoral popliteal, posterior tibial
+ dorsalis pedis.

GIS NAD

GUS NAD

CNS Loss of lumbar lordosis, spasm of R erector spinae.
Straight leg raising R restricted to 45°.
Reflexes present & equal. Neurol – depressed R ankle jerk.

IMMEDIATE PAST HISTORY
Paracetamol helped a little with previous intermittent back pain.

POINTS OF NOTE
Carpenter – active work.
1.78m, 68kg – tall, slightly-built

INVESTIGATIONS
MRI scan – narrowing of disc space between lumbar 4 & 5.

DIAGNOSIS
Prolapsed intervertebral disc.

MANAGEMENT
dihydrocodeine 30 mg 2 q.d.s p.c.
Bed rest, physio

Task 4

a) 6 hrly
b) for pain
c) 100 tablets
d) dihydrocodeine BP
e) give
f) tablets
g) write/label
h) after food/meals

Task 5

1 tablets
2 two
3 six
4 after
5 food/meals
6 can
7 pain

Task 6

1 Patient 3
2 Patient 6
3 Patient 5
4 Patient 2
5 Patient 1
6 Patient 7
7 Patient 4

a) twice a day
b) three times a day
c) with food
d) in the morning

Task 7

1 d 2 b 3 e 4 c 5 a

Task 8

1 You should lie on a hard surface.
2 You should be careful while getting out of bed. Try to roll over and then get up from your side.
3 You should (try to) avoid bending forward, for example, if you are picking up something off the floor.
4 You should try to bend your knees and keep your back straight.
5 You should (try to) avoid lifting heavy weights.

Task 11

Sheet No. ......1...... *Please use a ball point pen*

PRESCRIPTION SHEET

ORAL and OTHER NON-PARENTERAL MEDICINES – REGULAR PRESCRIPTIONS

CODE	Date Com-menced	MEDICINES (*Block Letters*)	DOSE	Method of Admin.	AM 6	AM 8	AM 10	MD 12	PM 2	PM 6	PM 10	MN 12	Other Times		DOCTOR'S SIGNATURE	Discontinued Date	Discontinued Initials
A	15/9/97	ASPIRIN	300 mg	p.o.		x											
B	"	PARACETAMOL	1 g	p.o.		x		x		x	x						
C	"	TEMAZEPAM	20 mg	p.o.							x						
D	"	ATENOLOL	100 mg	p.o.		x											
E	"	ISOSORBIDE MONONITRATE m/r	60 mg	p.o.		x											
F	"	THYROXINE	0.1 mg	p.o.		x											
G	"	GTN PUMP SPRAY	400–800 μg	s.l.										p.r.n.			
H	"	AMLODIPINE	5 mg	p.o.		x											
I	"	BENDROFLUAZIDE	2.5 mg	p.o.		x											
J	"																
K																	
L																	

PARENTERAL MEDICINES – REGULAR PRESCRIPTIONS

CODE	Date Com-menced	MEDICINES	DOSE	Method of Admin.	AM 6	AM 8	AM 10	MD 12	PM 2	PM 6	PM 10	MN 12	Other Times		DOCTOR'S SIGNATURE	Discontinued Date	Discontinued Initials
M	"	HEPARIN SODIUM	5000u	S.C.		x			x		x						
N	"	DIAMORPHINE	5 mg	IM									4 hrly	p.r.n.			
O	"	CYCLIZINE	50 mg	IM									4 hrly	p.r.n.			
P																	
Q																	

PLEASE ✔ WHEN MEDICINES ARE PRESCRIBED ON

Fluid (Additive Medicine) Prescription Chart	
Diabetic Chart	
Anticoagulant Chart	
Anaesthetic Prescription Sheet	
Record of Labour Sheet	

If medicine discontinued because of suspected adverse reaction please enter in box below

MEDICINE	ADVERSE REACTION
1	
2	

DIET

Date	DETAILS	Initials

ORAL and OTHER NON-PARENTERAL MEDICINES – ONCE ONLY PRESCRIPTIONS

Date	MEDICINE	DOSE	Method of Admin.	Time of Admin.•	DOCTOR'S SIGNATURE	Given by Initials	Time if Diff.*

ORAL and OTHER NON-PARENTERAL MEDICINES – ONCE ONLY PRESCRIPTIONS

Date	MEDICINE	DOSE	Method of Admin.	Time of Admin.•	DOCTOR'S SIGNATURE	Given by Initials	Time if Diff.*

NAME OF PATIENT	AGE	UNIT NUMBER	CONSULTANT	KNOWN DRUG/MEDICINE SENSITIVITY
WYNNE, John	58	1563526	MR SWAN	

Discharge Summary (page 2)

OPERATION:	CABG x4, single saphenous grafts to LAD and RCA, sequential saphenous graft to OM1 and OM2.
SURGEON:	A. Swan Assistant: Mr Dickson GA: Dr Wood
INCISIONS:	Median sternotomy and right thigh and leg.
FINDINGS:	Dense inferior left ventricular scarring, less marked scarring of inferior right ventricle. Fair overall left ventricular contraction. Diffuse coronary artery disease. All vessels measuring about 1.5 mm in diameter.
PUMP PERFUSION DATA:	Membrane oxygenator, linear flow, aortic SVC and IVC cannulae, LV apical vent. Whole body cooling to 28°C, cold cardioplegic arrest and topical cardiac hypothermia for the duration of the aortic cross clamp. Aortic cross clamp time 54 minutes, total bypass time 103 minutes.
PROCEDURE:	Vein was prepared for use as grafts. Systemic heparin was administered and bypass established, the left ventricle was vented, the aorta was cross-clamped and cold cardioplegic arrest of the heart obtained. Topical cooling was continued for the duration of the aortic cross clamp. Attention was first turned to the first and second obtuse marginal branches of the circumflex coronary artery. The first obtuse marginal was intramuscular with proximal artheroma. It admitted a 1.5 mm occluder and was grafted with saphenous sequential grafts, side to side using continuous 6/0 special prolene which was used for all subsequent distal anastomoses. The end of this saphenous graft was recurved and anastomosed to the second obtuse marginal around a 1.75 mm occluder. The left anterior descending was opened in its distal half and accepted a 1.5 mm occluder around which it was grafted with a single length of long saphenous vein. Lastly, the right coronary artery was opened at the crux and again grafted with a single length of saphenous vein around a 1.5 mm occluder whilst the circulation was rewarmed. The aortic cross clamp was released and air vented from the left heart and ascending aorta. Proximal vein anastomoses to the ascending aorta were completed using continuous 5/0 prolene. The heart was defibrillated into sinus rhythm with a single counter shock and weaned off bypass with minimal adrenalin support. Protamine sulphate was administered and blood volume was adjusted. Cannulae were removed and cannulation and vent sites repaired. Haemostasis was ascertained. Pericardial and mediastinal argyle drains were inserted.
CLOSURE:	Routine layered closure with ethibond to sternum, dexon to presternal and subcutaneous tissues, subcuticular dexon to skin.

A. Swan

Task 14

1 coronary artery bypass graft
2 left anterior descending
3 right coronary artery
4 first obtuse marginal
5 left ventricle/ventricular

Task 16

A Freetext	*B MeSH term*
1 drug	pharmaceutical preparations
2 treatment	therapy, therapeutics
3 baldness	alopecia
4 limb	extremities
5 stroke	cerebrovascular accident
6 heart attack	myocardial infarction
7 bleeding nose	epistaxis
8 athlete's foot	tinea pedis
9 boils	furunculosis
10 blood poisoning	septicemia
11 cancer	neoplasms
12 miscarriage	abortion, spontaneous

Task 17

1 treatment AND cluster headaches
2 lung neoplasms AND non-smokers AND incidence
Select Gender:male from the *Limits* menus
3 therapy AND nasal furunculosis
4 neurological damage AND sheep farmers AND organophosphorous pesticides
5 disease risk AND birds NOT pigeons
6 asbestosis AND shipyard workers
7 risk AND breast neoplasms AND hormone-replacement therapy AND oestrogens NOT oestrogen–progestogen
8 tattoos AND hepatitis
9 cannabis AND amnesia
10 cholesterol reduction AND statins

Task 18

Abstract	*Citation*
A	2
B	4
C	5
D	3

Appendix 1

Language functions

Case-taking

General information / Personal details

What's your name?
How old are you?
What's your job?
Where do you live?
Are you married?
Do you smoke?
How many do you smoke each day?
Do you drink?
Beer, wine or spirits? (UK)
Beer, wine or alcohol? (US)

PRESENT ILLNESS

Starting the interview

What's brought you along today?
What can I do for you?
What seems to be the problem?
How can I help?

Asking about duration

How long have they/has it been bothering you?
How long have you had them/it?
When did they/it start?

Asking about location

Where does it hurt?
Where is it sore?
Show me where the problem is.
Which part of your (head) is affected?
Does it stay in one place or does it go anywhere else?

Asking about type of pain and severity of problem

What's the pain like?
What kind of pain is it?
Can you describe the pain?
Is it bad enough to (wake you up)?
Does it affect your work?
Is it continuous or does it come and go?
How long does it last?

Asking about relieving or aggravating factors

Is there anything that makes it better/worse?
Does anything make it better/worse?

Asking about precipitating factors

What seems to bring it on?
Does it come on at any particular time?

Asking about medication

Have you taken anything for it?
Did (the tablets) help?

Asking about other symptoms

Apart from your (headaches) are there any other problems?

Previous health / Past history

How have you been keeping up to now?
Have you ever been admitted to hospital?
Have you ever had (headaches) before?
Has there been any change in your health since your last visit?

Family history

Are your parents alive and well?
What did he/she die of?
How old was he/she?
Does anyone else in your family suffer from this problem?

Asking about systems

Have you any trouble with (passing water)?
Any problems with (your chest)?
What's (your appetite) like?
Have you noticed any (blood in your stools)?
Do you ever suffer from (headaches)?
Do (bright lights) bother you?
Have you (a cough)?

To rephrase if the patient does not understand, try another way of expressing the same function, for example:

What caused this?
What brought this on?
Was it something you tried to lift?

Examination

Preparing the patient

I'm just going to (test your reflexes).
I'd just like to (examine your mouth).
Now I'm going to (tap your arm).
I'll just check your (blood pressure).

Instructing the patient

Would you (strip to the waist), please?
Can you (put your hands on your hips)?
Could you (bend down and touch your toes)?
Now I just want to see you (walking).
Lift it up as far as you can go, will you?
Let me see you (standing).

Checking if information is accurate

That's tender?

Down here?

The back of your leg?

Confirming information you know

That's tender.

Down here.

The back of your leg.

Commenting/reassuring

I'm checking your (heart) now.
That's fine.
OK, we've finished now.

Investigations

Explaining purpose

I'm going to (take a sample of your bone marrow) to find out what's causing (your anaemia).

Reassuring

It won't take long.
It won't be sore.
I'll be as quick as I can.

Warning

You may feel (a bit uncomfortable).
You'll feel a (jab).

Discussing investigations

Essential	*Possibly useful*	*Not required*
should must be + required essential important indicated	could	need not be + not necessary not required not important
Essential not to do		
should not must not be + contraindicated		

Making a diagnosis

Discussing certainty

	Certain	*Fairly certain*	*Uncertain*
Yes	is must	seems probably likely	might could may
No	can't definitely not exclude rule out	unlikely	possibly a possibility

EXPLAINING THE DIAGNOSIS

Simple definition

The (disc) is a (little pad of gristle between the bones in your back).

Cause and effect

If we bend the knee, tension is taken off the nerve.
When we straighten it, the nerve goes taut.

TREATMENT

Advising

I *advise* you to give up smoking.
You'll *have to* cut down on fatty foods.
You *must* rest.
You *should* sleep on a hard mattress.
If you *get up*, all your weight will press down on the disc.
Don't sit up to eat.

Expressing regret

I'm afraid that (the operation has not been successful).
I'm sorry to have to tell you that (your father has little chance of recovery).

Appendix 2

Common medical abbreviations

AB	apex beat
abdo.	abdomen
abdms (M)(t)(o)	abdomen without masses, tenderness, organomegaly (US)
a.c.	before meals
ACTH	adrenocorticotrophic hormone
AF	atrial fibrillation
AFP	alphafoetoprotein
A:G	albumen globulin ratio
AHA	Area Health Authority (UK)
AI	aortic incompetence
AJ	ankle jerk
a.m.	morning
AN	antenatal
AP	antero-posterior
APH	antepartum haemorrhage
ARM	artificial rupture of membranes
AS	alimentary system
ASD	atrial septal defect
ASHD	arteriosclerotic heart disease (US)
ASO	antistreptolysin O
ATS	antitetanic serum
A & W	alive and well
AMA	American Medical Association
BB	bed bath; blanket bath
BC	bone conduction
b.d.	twice a day
BF	breast fed
BI	bone injury
BID	brought in dead
b.i.d.	twice a day
BIPP	bismuth iodoform and paraffin paste
BM	bowel movement
BMA	British Medical Association
BMR	basal metabolic rate
BNF	British National Formulary
BNO	bowels not opened
BO	bowels opened
BP	blood pressure
BPC	British Pharmaceutical Codex
BPD	bi-parietal diameter
BS	breath sounds; bowel sounds
BUN	blood urea nitrogen (US)
BWt	birth weight

c̄	with
C	head presentation
Ca.	cancer; carcinoma
CAD	coronary artery disease
Capt.	head presentation
CAT	coaxial or computerised axial tomography
CABG	coronary artery bypass graft
CBC	complete blood count (US)
c.c.	with food
CCF	congestive cardiac failure (UK)
Chr.CF	chronic cardiac failure
Cf.	first certificate (UK)
CF	final certificate (UK)
CFT	complement fixation test
CHF	chronic heart failure; congestive heart failure (US)
CNS	central nervous system
CO	casualty officer (UK)
c/o	complains of
COAD	chronic obstructive airways disease (UK)
COP	change of plaster
COPD	chronic obstructive pulmonary disease (US)
CPN	community psychiatric nurse (UK)
creps	crepitations (UK) (râles US)
C-section	cesarean section (US)
CSF	cerebrospinal fluid
CSSD	Central Sterile Supply Depot (UK)
CSU	catheter specimen of urine
CT	cerebral tumour; coronary thrombosis
CV	cardiovascular
CVA	cardiovascular accident; cerebrovascular accident
CVS	cardiovascular system; cerebrovascular system
Cx	cervix
CXR	chest X-ray
D	divorced
D & C	dilatation and curettage
DD	dangerous drugs
DDA	Dangerous Drugs Act (UK)
decub.	lying down
DIC	drunk in charge
dl	decilitre
DN	District Nurse (UK)
DNA	did not attend
DOA	dead on arrival
DRO	Disablement Resettlement Office (UK)
DS	disseminated sclerosis
DTs	delirium tremens
DU	duodenal ulcer
DVT	deep venous thrombosis
D & V	diarrhoea and vomiting
DWP	Department for Work and Pensions (UK)
△/Dx	diagnosis
E	electrolytes
ECF	extracellular fluid
ECG/EKG(US)	electrocardiogram
ECT	electroconvulsive therapy
EDC	expected date of confinement

EDD	expected date of delivery
EDM	early diastolic murmur
EEG	electroencephalogram
ENT	ear, nose and throat
ESN	educationally sub-normal
ESR	erythrocyte sedimentation rate
ETT	exercise tolerance test
EUA	examination under anaesthesia
F	female
fb	finger breadth
FB	foreign body
FBC	full blood count (UK)
FH	foetal heart
FHH	foetal heart heard
FHNH	foetal heart not heard
fl	femtolitre
FMFF	foetal movement first felt
FPC	family planning clinic (UK)
FTAT	fluorescent treponemal antibody test
FTBD	fit to be detained; full term born dead
FTND	full term normal delivery
FUO	fever of unknown origin
g	gram
GA	general anaesthetic
GB	gall bladder
GC	general condition
GCFT	gonococcal complement fixation test
GIS	gastro-intestinal system
GOT	glumatic oxaloacetic transaminase
GP	General Practitioner (UK)
GPI	general paralysis of the insane
GPT	glutamic pyruvic transaminase
GTN	glyceryl trinitrate
GTT	glucose tolerance test
GU	gastric ulcer
GUS	genito-urinary system
Gyn.	gynaecology
Hb/Hgb	haemoglobin
HBP	high blood pressure
Hct	haematocrit
H & P	history and physical examination
HP	house physician (UK)
HR	heart rate
HS	heart sounds
IBS	irritable bowel syndrome
ICF	intracellular fluid
ICS	intercostal space
ID	infectious disease
IM	intramuscular
IOFB	intra-ocular foreign body
IP	in-patient; interphalangeal
IQ	intelligence quotient
ISQ	in statu quo
IU	international unit

IV	intravenous
IVC	inferior vena cava
IVP	intravenous pyelogram
IVU	intravenous urogram
Ix	investigation
IZS	insulin zinc suspension
JVD	jugular venous distention (US)
JVP	jugular venous pressure (UK)
KUB	kidney, ureter and bladder
L	left
LA	left atrium; local anaesthetic
LAD	left axis deviation; left anterior descending
LBP	low back pain; low blood pressure
LDH	lactic dehydrogenase
LE cells	lupus erythematosus cells
LFTS	liver function tests
LHA	Local Health Authority (UK)
LIF	left iliac fossa
LIH	left inguinal hernia
LKS	liver, kidney and spleen
LLL	left lower lobe
LLQ	left lower quadrant
LMN	lower motor neurone
LMP	last menstrual period; left mento-posterior position of foetus
LOA	left occipito-anterior position of foetus
LOP	left occipito-posterior position of foetus
LP	lumbar puncture
LSCS	lower segment caesarean section
LUA	left upper arm
LUQ	left upper quadrant
LV	left ventricle; lumbar vertebra
LVD	left ventricular dysfunction
LVE	left ventricular enlargement
LVF	left ventricular failure
LVH	left ventricular hypertrophy
M	male
mane	in the morning
M/F; M/W/S	male/female; married/widow(er)/single
MCD	mean corpuscular diameter
MCH	mean corpuscular haemoglobin
MCHC	mean corpuscular haemoglobin concentration
MCL	mid-clavicular line
MCV	mean corpuscular volume
MDM	mid-diastolic murmur
mg	milligram
MI	mitral incompetence insufficiency; myocardial infarction
Mitte	give
ml	millilitre
MMR	mass miniature radiography; measles, mumps & rubella vaccination
MO	Medical Officer (UK)
MOH	Medical Officer of Health (UK)
MOP	medical out-patient
m/r	modified release

MRC	Medical Research Council (UK)
MRI	magnetic resonance imaging
MS	mitral stenosis; multiple sclerosis; musculo skeletal
MSU	mid-stream urine
MSSU	mid-stream specimen of urine
MSW	Medical Social Worker (UK)
MVP	mitral valve prolapse
NA	not applicable
NAD	no abnormality detected
NBI	no bone injury
ND	normal delivery
NE	not engaged
NIC	National Insurance Certificate (UK)
NND	neo-natal death
nocte	at night
NOF	neck of femur
NP	not palpable
NPU	not passed urine
NS	nervous system
NSA	no significant abnormality
NSPCC	National Society for the Prevention of Cruelty to Children (UK)
NYD	not yet diagnosed
OA	on admission; osteo-arthritis
OAP	old age pensioner
OBS	organic brain syndrome
Obs	obstetrics
O/E	on examination
oed.	oedema
OM	otitis media
OR	operating room (US)
OT	operating theatre (UK)
P	pulse; protein
Para. 2 + 1	full term pregnancies 2, abortions 1
PAT	paroxysmal atrial tachycardia
PBI	protein bound iodine
p.c.	after food
PDA	patent ductus arteriosus
PERLA	pupils equal and reactive to light and accommodation
PET	pre-eclamptic toxaemia
PID	prolapsed intervertebral disc; pelvic inflammatory disease
Pl.	plasma
p.m.	afternoon
PM	postmortem
PMB	postmenopausal bleeding
PN	postnatal
PND	postnatal depression; paroxysmal nocturnal dyspnoea
PO2	pressure of oxygen
p.o.	by mouth
POP	plaster of Paris
PPH	postpartum haemorrhage
p.r.	per rectum
p.r.n.	as required
PROM	premature rupture of membranes
PSW	Psychiatric Social Worker (UK)

PU	passed urine; peptic ulcer
PUO	pyrexia of unknown or uncertain origin
p.v.	per vaginam
PVT	paroxysmal ventricular tachycardia
PZI	protamine zinc insulin
q.d.s./q.i.d.	four times a day
R	right; respiration; red
R_X	take (used in prescriptions)
RA	rheumatoid arthritis; right atrium
RAD	right axis deviation
RBC	red blood cell count; red blood corpuscles
RBS	random blood sugar
RCA	right coronary artery
ref.	refer
reg.	regular
RGN	Registered General Nurse
Rh.	Rhesus factor; rheumatism
RHA	Regional Health Authority (UK)
RI	respiratory infection
RIF	right iliac fossa
RIH	right inguinal hernia
RLL	right lower lobe
RLQ	right lower quadrant
RMO	Regional or Resident Medical Offier (UK)
ROA	right occipital anterior
ROM	range of motion
ROP	right occipital posterior
RS	respiratory system
RTA	road traffic accident
RTC	return to clinic
RUA	right upper arm
RUQ	right upper quadrant
RTI	respiratory tract infection
RVE	right ventricular enlargement
RVH	right ventricular hypertrophy
Rx	treatment
S	single; sugar
SAH	subarachnoidal haemorrhage
SB	still-born
SBE	sub-acute bacterial endocarditis
s.c.	subcutaneous
sep.	separated
SG	specific gravity
SHO	Senior House Officer (UK)
SI	sacro-iliac
sig.	write / label (in prescriptions)
s.l.	sublingual
SM	systolic murmur
SMR	sub-mucous resection
SN	student nurse (UK)
SOB	short of breath
SOBOE	short of breath on exertion
SOP	surgical out-patients
SRN	State Registered Nurse (UK)

SROM	spontaneous rupture of membranes
STs	sanitary towels
SVC	superior vena cava
SVD	spontaneous vertex delivery
SWD	short wave diathermy
T	temperature
tabs	tablets
T & A	tonsils and adenoids
TB	tuberculosis
t.d.s./t.i.d.	three times daily
TI	tricuspid incompetence
TIA	transient ischaemic attack
TMJ	temporo mandibular joint
TNS	transcutaneous nerve stimulator
TOP	termination of pregnancy
TPHA	treponema pallidum haemagglutination
TPR	temperature, pulse, respiration
TR	temporary resident (UK)
TS	tricuspid stenosis
TSH	thyroid stimulating hormone
TT	tetanus toxoid; tuberculin tested
TV	trichomonas vaginalis
TURP	transurethral prostate resection
U	urea
U & E	urea and electrolytes
UGS	urogenital system
UMN	upper motor neurone
URTI	upper respiratory tract infection
USP	United States Pharmacopeic
USS	ultrasound scan
UVL	ultra-violet light
VD	venereal disease
VDRL	venereal disease research laboratory
VE	vaginal examination
VI	virgo intacta
VP	venous pressure
VSD	ventricular septal defect
VV	varicose vein(s)
Vx	vertex
W	widow/widower
WBC	white blood cell count; white blood corpuscles
WNL	within normal limits
WR	Wassermann reaction
XR	X-ray
YOB	year of birth
#	fracture

Appendix 3

Who's who in the British hospital system

CONSULTANT
The most senior position held by physicians or surgeons with the highest qualifications, e.g. FRCS, MRCP, and who have completed a programme of higher specialist training.*

SPECIALIST REGISTRAR
A position held by a doctor with the highest degree in a chosen speciality who is following a programme of higher specialist training to enable him or her to be included on the Specialist Register. Inclusion on this register makes the doctor eligible for consultant posts.*

ASSOCIATE SPECIALIST
A senior position where the holder is responsible to a named consultant. Associate Specialists must have at least 10 years' experience since registration but are not required to have a higher qualification and do not proceed to consultant level.

STAFF DOCTOR
A doctor who exercises an intermediate level of clinical responsibility as delegated by consultants. Staff doctors do not proceed to consultant level.

SENIOR HOUSE OFFICER
A one year appointment (usually residential) held by a doctor who is studying for a higher qualification.

HOUSE OFFICER
A position held by a doctor who has completed the pre-registration year.

PRE-REGISTRATION HOUSE OFFICER
A position held by a newly qualified doctor for one year, prior to full registration.

DIRECTOR OF NURSING SERVICES
The most senior position in nursing administration.

MATRON
A senior sister accountable for a group of wards.

NURSE SPECIALIST
A nurse with specialist expertise in education and support for particular groups of patients, e.g. those with kidney transplants, cancer or diabetes.

SENIOR NURSE
A senior management position.

DEPARTMENTAL SISTER
A senior position for a nurse with experience and either SRN or RGN (three years' training).

WARD SISTER
A qualified and experienced nurse with overall responsibility for a ward.

STAFF NURSE
First post for a SRN/RGN qualified nurse.

NURSING AUXILIARY/NURSING ASSISTANT
Untrained nursing assistants.

*Note that Consultants and Specialist Registrars who are surgeons drop the title Dr and are addressed as Mr/Mrs/Ms/Miss.

Appendix 4

A broad equivalence of positions in the NHS and US hospital systems

NHS Hospital	*US Hospital*
Consultant	Attending Physician
Specialist Registrar	Senior Resident
Associate Specialist	
Staff Grade	
Senior House Officer	Resident
Pre-registration House Officer	Intern

Appendix 5

Useful addresses

UK and Ireland

British Medical Association
BMA House
Tavistock Square
London WC1H 9JP
www.bma.org.uk

International Department
www.bma.org.uk/international

Nursing and Midwifery Council
23 Portland Place
London W1B 1PZ
www.nmc-uk.org

Department of Health
Richmond House
79 Whitehall
London SW1A 2NL
www.dh.gov.uk

Faculty of Accident and Emergency Medicine
35–43 Lincoln's Inn Fields
London WC2A 3PE
www.faem.org.uk

General Medical Council
178 Great Portland Street
London W1W 5JE
www.gmc-uk.org

Medical Defence Union
230 Blackfriars Road
London SE1 8PJ
www.the-mdu.com

Medical and Dental Defence Union of Scotland
Mackintosh House,
120 Blythswood Street
Glasgow G2 4EA
www.mddus.com

Medical Protection Society Ltd
33 Cavendish Square
London W1G 0PS
www.mps.org.uk

Medical Research Council
20 Park Crescent
London W1N 3PA
www.mrc.ac.uk

Royal College of Anaesthetists
48–49 Russell Square
London W1B 1AL
www.rcoa.ac.uk

Royal College of General Practitioners
14 Princes Gate
Hyde Park
London SW7 1PU
www.rcgp.org.uk

Royal College of Midwives
15 Mansfield Street
London W1G 9NH
www.rcm.org.uk

Royal College of Obstetricians and Gynaecologists
27 Sussex Place
Regent's Park
London NW1 4RG
www.rcog.org.uk

Royal College of Ophthalmologists
17 Cornwall Terrace
London NW1 4QW
www.rcophth.ac.uk

Royal College of Paediatrics and Child Health
50 Hallam Street
London W1W 6DE
www.rcph.ac.uk

Royal College of Physicians of Edinburgh
9 Queen Street
Edinburgh EH2 1JQ
www.rcpe.ac.uk

Royal College of Physicians of Ireland
6 Kildare Street,
Dublin D2
Ireland
www.rcpi.ie/

Royal College of Physicians of London
11 St Andrew's Place
Regent's Park
London NW1 4LE
www.rcplondon.ac.uk

Royal College of Surgeons of Edinburgh
Nicolson Street
Edinburgh EH8 9DW
www.rcsed.ac.uk

Royal College of Surgeons of England
35–43 Lincoln's Inn Fields
London WC2A 3PE
www.rcseng.ac.uk

Royal College of Surgeons in Ireland
St Stephen's Green
Dublin D2
www.rcsi.ie/

USA

American Medical Association
515 N State Street
Chicago IL 60610
www.ama-assn.org

American Academy of Family Physicians
PO Box 11210
Shawnee Mission
KS 66207-1210
www.aafp.org

American College of Physicians
109 N Independence Mall W
Philadelphia PA 19106-1572
www.acponline.org

American College of Surgeons
633 N Saint Clair Street
Chicago IL 60611-3211
www.facs-org/

American Hospital Association
One North Franklin
Chicago IL 60606-3421
www.hospitalconnect.com

Educational Commission for Foreign Medical Graduates
3624 Market Street
Philadelphia PENN 19104-2685
www.ecfmg.org

Southern Medical Association
35 Lakeshore Drive
Birmingham AL 35209
www.sma.org

Supplementary activities

1 *Exploiting case histories*

Case histories provide a rich source of materials and can be found in journals across a wide range of specialisations. They can also be found in practice booklets for Royal College exams. They can be exploited in many ways. As a starting point for authentic problem-solving activity they lend themselves naturally to task-based learning.

Here are a few suggestions:

To develop reading skills

For example, a simple scanning activity (see Unit 1 Task 11).

As a starting point for information-transfer activities

One mode of text is transferrred to another text type, for example, where information from a case report is transformed into case notes or vice versa, or used as a source of information for the completion of a form or a letter (see Unit 5 Task 15).

As the basis for a role-play

For example, pairs of students are given different case reports from which they take case notes and use them as the basis for doctor/patient role-play. The person taking the role of the doctor takes notes which can be compared with the 'patient's notes' at the end of the session. At the examination stage the 'doctor' gives an indication of the examinations and investigations felt to be appropriate and is given the results requested. Diagnosis and treatment are then discussed and the explanation stage role-played. It is usually more productive if there are preparation stages to the role-play. This involves students who will play the same role working together on the language and questions before entering the role-play stage as this allows for a more focused approach to the use of appropriate language.

2 *Using the learner as a source*

Doctors can produce their own case histories to work from. These provide a bank of material which can be used with future groups. The student role-plays can also be videoed or recorded for use in listening activities with other students.

Recordings of descriptions/instructions/explanations of different examinations done in pairs (perhaps in another room) can be played back to the class for listening purposes, for example, deciding what the examination/investigation is, the kind of conditions that might be being considered, how the patient might be managed, etc.

3 *Other language work activities based on forms or case notes*

For example, abbreviation work (see Unit 1 Task 6) and question forms (see Unit 1 Task 2, Unit 2 Task 7).

4 *Cloze exercises*

See Unit 6 Task 12.

5 *Work on medical articles*

See Unit 5 Tasks 13 and 14, Unit 6 Tasks 11 and 12.
The same techniques can be applied to any journal articles. It is also useful to examine the different structure of articles and the criteria adopted.

6 *CDs, videos and audio cassettes*

These can be borrowed from medical libraries and exploited in a variety of ways, for example, as a basis for role-plays, note-taking and report-writing.

7 *Computer programmes*

Authoring packages such as Gapmaster (Wida Software) allow you to put short texts, e.g. case histories, on disk and create cloze passages with assistance and a scoring system. The students find these exercises very motivating and it can work very well as a group activity. Different groups can work on different cases and once the texts are complete they can be used like any other text, for example, as the basis for note-taking activities, role-plays and information-transfer activities.

8 *Jigsaw reading and listening activities*

A text can be divided into two or three parts and either photocopied or recorded. A common worksheet provides the basis of a task where the texts are either listened to or read in different groups. The groups are then reorganised for an information exchange to allow for task completion.

9 *Read and report*

Students are either given or allowed to choose short texts which they then summarise for other students to take notes on.

10 *Triads*

These develop skimming, scanning, note-taking, listening and presentation skills.

Students are given a pile of journals and they have ten minutes to select and summarise an article or piece of text. The time limit is critical and they should be encouraged to choose short articles. They are then organised into groups of three and ascribed a role.

Phase 1

Student A is presenter
Student B is reporter
Student C is observer

Stage 1	A presents B and C take notes
Stage 2	B gives a summary of A's presentation while C listens
Stage 3	C comments on B's summary and adds anything that has been missed out
Stage 4	All three compare notes

Phase 2

Student C becomes presenter
Student A becomes reporter
Student B becomes observer

The procedure is repeated following the four stages listed above.

Phase 3

Student B becomes presenter
Student C becomes reporter
Student A becomes observer

Although it is rather tricky to set this activity up the first time, if it is done on a regular basis the students become much more efficient in following the procedures. There is always a marked improvement in their presentation skills which makes it a really worthwhile exercise. There is also a noticeable improvement in the article selection, as an awareness of audience interest and motivation increases.

11 *Group presentations*

These usually work better than individual presentations as they tend to be more lively and active. It is also quite useful to video them so that feedback is more instant. The use of PowerPoint or slides is also invaluable for this kind of activity. Encouraging the audience to participate in note-taking activities or some kind of observation task helps to make the whole experience a more fruitful one.

12 *Project presentations*

These are becoming a very important way of sharing research and development ideas at national and international conferences. If the students are divided into groups they have time for data collection through reading, questionnaires, videos, audio tapes or interviews. They then produce a poster which may be of a very visual nature. These are put up around the room for all to view in advance of the presentations. The presentation sessions should be kept very brief and should involve the whole group taking it in turns to speak. This is followed by a question and answer session. It is helpful if the group have some time before to anticipate questions and discuss how they might answer them before the sessions. This kind of group activity is very good for building students' confidence and is well worth the effort. Again, if these sessions can be videoed, feedback can be immediate and extremely useful. Videoed sessions also make very good listening material for future groups.

13 *Case presentations*

It is possible to get hold of taped and videotaped case presentations. Another good starting point would be to get students to work on case presentations of William Hudson, the case history that runs through *English in Medicine*.

14 *Diagnostic problems and quizzes*

Many magazines such as *GP Magazine*, *Pulse* and *Mims*, which are produced for British doctors have short problems and quizzes which can be put onto cards for self-access, role-play, or simply as straightforward problem-solving activities. Many of them have good photographic input which can be very good for vocabulary development.

15 *Authentic documents*

There are quite a few of these in *English in Medicine* and they can be used in different contexts and in different ways. Magazines produced for native-speaker doctors can also be a good source for these.

16 *Medline*

Medline provides a rich source for research-based activities.

Acknowledgements

The authors and publishers are grateful to the following for permission to reproduce copyright material. It has not always been possible to identify the sources of all the material used and in such cases the publishers would welcome information from the copyright owners.

Elsevier for the extract on p. 13 from *Illustrated Cases in Acute Clinical Medicine*, p. 31, by K. C. McHardy et al., © Elsevier 1994, for the extract on p. 25 on angina from *Davidson's Principles and Practice of Medicine*, 17th edition, p. 248, © Elsevier 1995, and for the extract on p. 69 from *Outline of Orthopaedics*, 10th Edition, p. 217, by J. C. Adams, © Elsevier 1986; p. 25 The McGraw-Hill Companies for the extract on pericarditis from *Harrison's Principles of Internal Medicine*, 13th Edition, pp. 1094–5, by K. J. Isselbacker et al., © 1994 The McGraw-Hill Companies; pp. 34–5 BMJ Publishing Group for the extracts from the *British National Formulary*, Joint Formulary Committee, *British National Formulary,* 47th ed., London: British Medical Association and Royal Pharmaceutical Society of Great Britain, 2004. This material has been reproduced from the BNF solely to test the ability to extract relevant information; the reproduced information is incomplete and on its own unsuitable for clinical decision-making. The information on the use of medicines changes constantly: the BNF is revised each March and September and consequently the citation is out-of-date; pp. 46—7 American Medical Association for the extracts from 'Improving Participation and Interrater Agreement in Scoring Ambulatory Pediatric Association Abstracts' from *Archives of Pediatric and Adolescent Medicine*, Vol. 150, pp. 380–3, April 1996, by K. J. Kemper et al., © 1996, American Medical Association; pp. 61–2 Elsevier for the extracts from 'Medical Research Council randomised trial of endometrial resection versus hysterectomy in management of menorrhagia' by Hugh Connor et al. from *The Lancet*, Vol. 349, March 29 1997, pp. 897–901, © 1997 Elsevier; pp. 71–4 British Journal of General Practice for the extracts from 'Gender differences in general practitioners at work' by Ruth Chambers and Ian Campbell from *British Journal of General Practice*, Vol. 46, No. 406, 1996, pp. 291–3, © *British Journal of General Practice*; p. 89 U.S. National Library of Medicine for the screenshot of the *Medline* online medical database PubMed summary page; p. 90 The Royal Society of Medicine for the screenshot from *Medline*, 'Homeopathic arnica for the prevention of pain and bruising in hand surgery' by Stevinson, Devaraj, Fountain-Barber, Hawkins and Ernst from *Journal of the Royal Society of Medicine*, 2003 February 96(2) 60–5, and for the screenshot from *Medline*, 'Clinical trail of homeopathic arnica C30 for pain and infection after total abdominal hysterectomy' by Mullee, Lewith and Miller from *Journal of the Royal Society of Medicine*, 1997 April 90(4): 239–40; p. 91 *British Journal of Oral and Maxillofacial Surgery* for the screenshot from *Medline*, 'Metronidazole (Flagyl) and Arnica Montana in the prevention of post-surgical complications' by G. S. Kaziro from *British Journal of Oral and Maxillofacial Surgery*, 1984 February: 22(1): 42–9; p. 92 InnoVision Communications for the screenshot from *Medline*, 'Use of arnica to relieve pain after carpal-tunnel release surgery' by Jeffrey and Belcher from *Alternative Therapies in Health and Medicine*, 2002 Mar–Apr; 8(2): 66–8.

For permission to reproduce photographs: p. 5 Corbis/Michael Keller; p. 15, 38, 65 Pulse Picture Library; p. 28 Corbis; p. 50 Science Photo Library/Simon Fraser / Royal Victoria Infirmary, Newcastle; p. 76 Getty Images/Comstock; p. 80 Science Photo Library/Larry Mulvehill; p. 82 Science Photo Library/Antonia Reeve

Photo research: Pictureresearch.co.uk

Cover image by Getty Images – Jonnie Miles.

Illustrations by Amanda MacPhail.

The recordings were produced by James Richardson at Studio AVP.